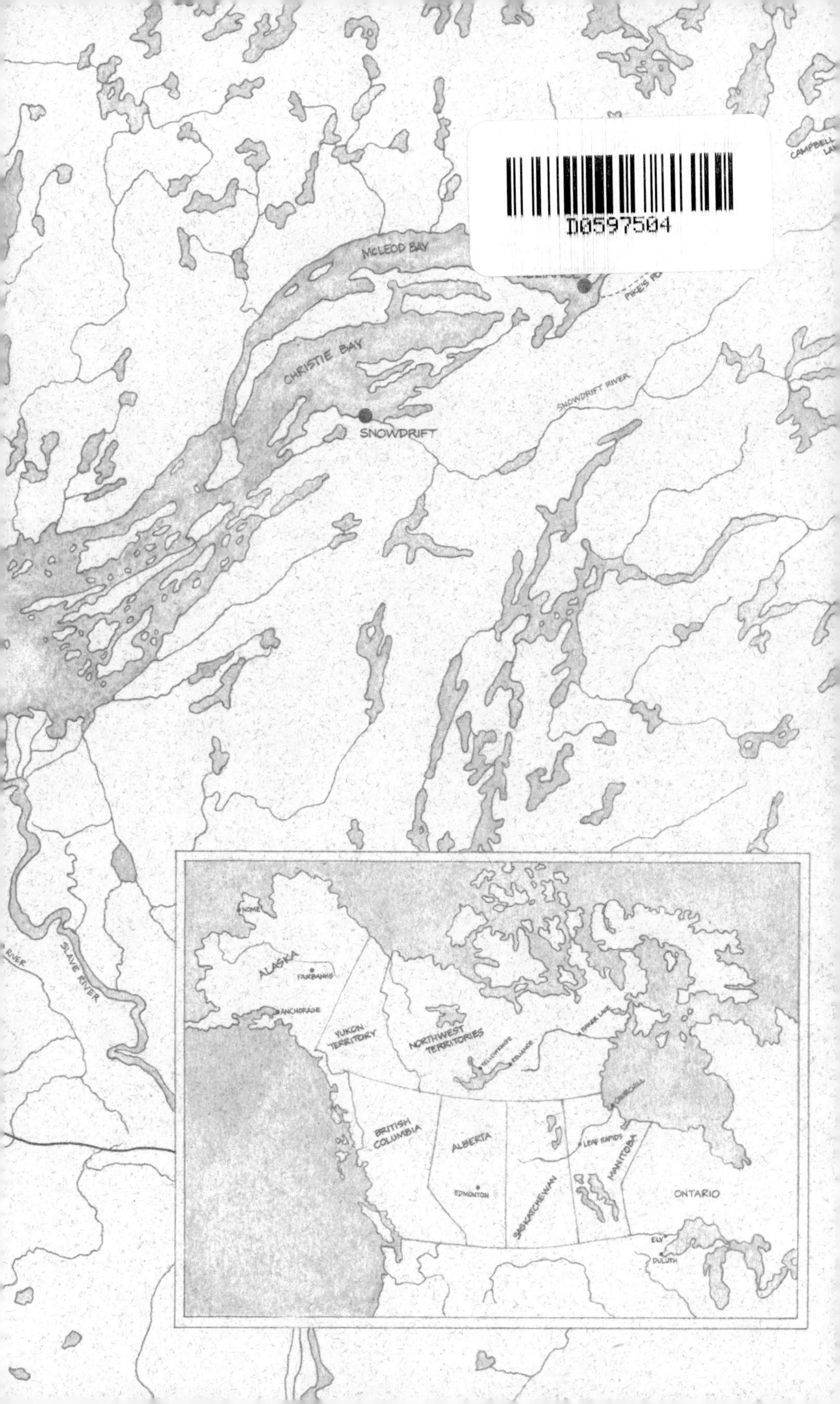
McLEOD BAY
CHRISTIE BAY
SNOWDRIFT
SNOWDRIFT RIVER
SLAVE RIVER
RIVER
NOME
ALASKA
FAIRBANKS
ANCHORAGE
YUKON TERRITORY
NORTHWEST TERRITORIES
YELLOWKNIFE
RELIANCE
BAKER LAKE
CHURCHILL
BRITISH COLUMBIA
ALBERTA
EDMONTON
SASKATCHEWAN
LEAF RAPIDS
MANITOBA
ONTARIO
ELY
DULUTH

COLD NIGHTS FAST TRAILS

REFLECTIONS OF A MODERN DOG MUSHER

COLD NIGHTS FAST TRAILS

REFLECTIONS OF A MODERN DOG MUSHER

Dave Olesen

NORTHWORD
PRESS, INC
BOX 1360, MINOCQUA, WI 54548

NorthWord Press, Inc.
Box 1360
Minocqua, WI 54548

For a Free Catalog describing NorthWord's line of nature books
and gifts, call 1-800-336-5666

ISBN 55971-041-1

For my grandfathers,
James M. Olesen and Herman E. Soderberg

ACKNOWLEDGMENTS

T HROUGHOUT THIS BOOK, I SPEAK ONLY FOR MYSELF and write only from the background of my own experiences, prejudices and opinions. This has, at times, seemed overly egotistical. I have kept in mind the words of Thoreau: "I should not talk so much about myself if there were anybody else whom I knew so well."

I should talk, too, about some of the people who have made long-distance dog mushing a part of my life. My parents, James and Linnea Olesen, have been supportive in ways that make that overused word sound completely inadequate. Fifteen years ago, neither of them would have known a dogsled from a wheelbarrow; now they urge me to persevere in mushing even at times when I am ready to call it quits. My wife, Kristen, appears only briefly in the stories that follow—for most of my first decade of mushing I was without her enthusiastic support, partnership and love. The dogs and I are lucky that we met her. She is serious about mushing and about our back-country life and her unfailing help has made possible the writing of this book.

There are many more people, some of them almost complete strangers to me still, who have made a difference for my dogs and me in the years and miles behind us. I thank all of you and look forward to sharing the trail, the road, or a visit with you again. Some of you are mentioned by name in these pages; most of you are not—but you are all there.

As a writer, I want to thank Tom Klein and everyone at NorthWord Press for making the publication process so painless. My friend and mentor, Lee Merrill, is a constant source of encouragement and Sam Cook of Duluth is an inspiration, a friend and an incisive critic. Of the most help, though, have been the authors and poets whose work has been so influential in my life—John Haines, Wendell Berry, William Stafford, Gary Snyder and many others. They have all had a lasting impact on my thinking and my decisions and thus upon my writing. I thank them.

Finally, there are those creatures around whom this entire book revolves and whom it sometimes sounds so corny to thank. My dogs, past and present and future, help me and put up with me and teach me and delight me. Thanks, all of you.

D.O.

INTRODUCTION

I JUST FINISHED READING DAVE OLESEN'S BOOK, *Cold Nights, Fast Trails,* while on a summer flight to the Midwest. Ground temperatures were about 78 degrees, but still I carried a feeling of snow on my shoes with Dave's stories fresh in my mind.

Perhaps I have an unfair advantage in being well able to visualize the wilderness and wolves, peaks and valleys of which Dave writes. I've raced with Dave and seen him out on the trail, putting red dog coats on his whole team, and had seen him in Nome when he went around with a pretty thoughtful expression on his wind-burnt face after surviving the worst snowstorm of his life.

Dave speaks of himself as not "writing from a pedestal of success" and here I would like to argue that he is wrong. After all, he has won both the sportsmanship award and the AK Airline Leon Hardseppala Humanitarian Award, two awards that a lot of Iditarod race "lifers" have never received. He has the most important kind of success—living a lifestyle he's chosen for himself, doing what he loves and continually improving, and having good people around him who teach and encourage him.

Cold Nights, Fast Trails is an account of northern lifestyle to the extreme, and the author touches many sides of it—the daily triumphs, the wild beauty, the pleasure of motion as the dogs run side by side, but also the hardships, the weather, the disappointments. And also the wondering that all of us have done who've lived this way (and not had a lobotomy) about why we put ourselves through it.

I found it refreshing to read the un-romanticized accounts of our sport of sled-dog racing, but at the same time, it reconfirmed a lot of the things I enjoy the most about it.

So, settle down in your favorite chair with your slippers and a blanket in some nice warm spot to read this book, and see if you finish it with a better understanding of why we'd freeze our knees for the pleasure of driving a sled dog team through some of the wildest, toughest land on the planet. I hope you enjoy this book as much as I did.

Libby Riddles
Iditarod Champion

PREFACE

WHEN TOM KLEIN OF NORTHWORD PRESS WROTE to me in December 1987 and suggested a book on long-distance dog mushing, he envisioned "not a how-to book, but a 'why' book . . . a sort of homage to the cult." That phrase has stuck in my mind throughout the writing of this book. Dog mushing is indeed, in these times, a cult. What was once a vital component of Northern life has evolved and re-emerged as sport, business and recreation. Like every cult worthy of the name, dog mushing has developed its own esoteric jargon, its own set of values and standards and a notable lack of conformity to the world "outside."

As I wrote, I was frequently tempted to make sweeping statements, to adopt the generalized "we" of dog mushers at large and to somehow put the diversity of methods and opinions into neat and predictable order. I did not always resist this temptation. It would be misleading, though, to convey to readers the impression of consistency within the realm of mushers and their dog-teams. Generalizations almost always fail in the attempt to convey the essence of sled dog work and sled dog people. For every sweeping statement, there seems to be an immediate rebuttal, equally true and completely opposite.

Dog mushing, especially as practiced in the form of long-distance races, has been and will remain somewhat controversial. The perception of dogs not as pets but as workers and fellow-athletes and the relationships between sled dogs and their mushers are difficult to convey to a public far removed from this perception and relationship. Here again I speak and write, only for myself and out of my own relationship with my dogteam. To those who regard the endeavor as cruel or ridiculous, I suggest a year of living, training, traveling and racing with a serious long-distance team. Then, if they have a judgment to make, it will at least be based in direct experience.

Unlike other musher-authors, I do not write from a pedestal of success. A vast majority of dog mushers will never stand on that honorable step, in Nome or Fairbanks, or at the North Pole, with their dogs. Yet we all continue to pursue our efforts with these teams of animals. I speak as one of the unknown majority, as an aspiring musher, one of the many who may never compete neck-and-neck on the trail with the best-known teams in the world, but who still gain experience and pay our dues, season after season. As my philosophical dog-musher friend Arleigh Jorgenson put it one morning, leaning on the handle of a shovel at the edge of his dog yard, "It's what Kierkegaard said—'the joy is in the becoming.'"

We are still *becoming,* my dogs and I, and like every other dogteam we always will be. The learning, adapting and experimenting never end. It is the joy and frustration and humor and excitement of this sled-dog life that I have tried to convey.

Still, there is the difficult question—"why?" When Tom Klein wrote to me, he was eager to know *why.* He wanted to publish a book that would answer that question. Days and miles and dogs and mushers—together they will form the following chapters. I hope that what will emerge is not an answer, but an understanding.

Dave Olesen
Hoarfrost River, Northwest Territories
Canada
15 May 1989

AUTHOR'S NOTE

All places, times, dates and facts herein are as accurate as memory and/or records can make them. All of the events I describe are true and all of the names of people and dogs are actual. At the risk of being run out of my adopted country, Canada, on a three-meter rail, I have given all weights in pounds, distances in miles and feet, and temperatures in degrees Fahrenheit.

CONTENTS

THE LIFE

IT IS CHRISTMAS NIGHT. AHEAD OF ME IN THE DARKNESS are the dim forms of eight running dogs, illumined by a slender crescent moon. It is cold, about −30 degrees. A rime of frost edges my face, where my breath smokes past the edge of my parka's ruff. Far ahead, faintly visible, rises the rugged north shore of McLeod Bay, at the far eastern end of Great Slave Lake.

A team of dogs, a sled, darkness and cold—we could be anywhere in the North, from the Yukon to Siberia, from Greenland to Alaska. We could be anywhere, but tonight we are nearing home, a tiny cluster of log buildings somewhere along that far shore. Ten miles to go.

I turn to look behind me, shifting my weight slightly on the runners of the big freight sled. I give a sharp slap to the switch on my left hip. Strapped over my thick fur cap is a headlamp and its bright beam pierces the darkness. A mile or so back, about halfway to the twin red lights on the radio tower at the Reliance Weather Station, another white light appears and shines steadily. My partner, Mike Dietzman, is following with another eight-dog team and his steady light is an answer to me, indicating that all is well. After five seconds or so, I switch my headlamp off again. His light goes out. As my eyes readjust to the darkness, I look straight down and can just make out a faint pattern of serrations in the snow—the telltale track of a snowmobile. Beaver still has the trail.

In an endeavor as fraught with romantic notions and clichés as the running of sled dogs, a person constantly faces the need to balance legend with reality. One of the persistent themes in the lore of arctic dog mushing is the uncanny ability of veteran lead dogs to find their way home, through all weather and without so much as a trace of the trail. As with most stereotypes, this notion falters a bit in the face of reality. Mike and I have often chuckled over it this season when our leaders—Beaver, McDougal and Banjo—have failed at times to live up to this overblown image of their talents. But tonight, Beaver is showing me his stuff and I am able to think with pride that without him out in front of this team, we would be having a dickens of a time making it home.

We cross to Reliance at sundown, which comes early at 62 degrees north latitude in late December. It is a cold run across the bay, but we are warm with anticipation. We arrive at the weather station in fading twilight at 3:30 in the afternoon, picket our teams on a long cable and head inside to the warmth and cheer of Christmas dinner with all the trimmings.

Six hours later, I walk out of the elaborately modern weather station building and take a sudden step back in time and downward in temperature. A stiff west wind is sweeping the 90-mile length of McLeod Bay and spitting tiny snowflakes from some thin broken clouds. It is cold, thoroughly dark after the bright lights indoors and quiet except for the rush of the wind and the muffled throb of the station's diesel generator. Christmas cheer has its work cut out for it.

There is no debate over whether to head back across the bay. In the morning, we would be on our way out, by ski-plane to Yellowknife. From there, we would begin the long drive south to the first race of the new season. We had worked all fall to get the team and the homestead ready for this departure. We would not miss it because of a little wind-drifted snow.

Mike is out the door behind me. With false bravado, we both hurry through the process of laying out harnesses and hooking up our teams. He helps me hitch a few dogs into place in my team, so that I would be ready to leave ahead of him. With a quick "Hike! Hike!", amidst the frenzy of barking and leaping dogs, Beaver and Troubles lead my crew out onto the ice. As we round Fairchild Point in a maze of old "Skidoo" tracks, I realize with grim surprise that the one trail we most need, our trail north 12 miles to home—had been nearly obliterated by blowing snow while we had been merrily stuffing ourselves with turkey and potatoes.

I keep my headlamp beam glued to the snow alongside the sled for a few tense minutes, watching closely for the occasional vestiges of old sled tracks. Soon it becomes clear that Beaver is not going to leave the trail and wander aimlessly out into the expanse of the bay. I turn my light off. As my eyes grow accustomed to the darkness, I realize that it is not as black a night as it had seemed at first. The moon is not yet down, the clouds are racing off to the east and behind them, the western sky is filled with stars.

A sudden blast of wind stings the tip of my nose. With a mittened hand I clumsily maneuver my soft woolen faceguard into place. My nose and chin have become sensitized to cold after two month's repeated blasts of frigid air and it seems I now spend half of every training run fiddling with my faceguard, moving it from my chin to my nose and back again.

The dogs are running well. At night there is always a heightened sense of speed when driving a team of dogs, especially in a forest where the trunks of trees pass at arm's length in the darkness. The quartering headwind here on the bay would account for a feeling of speed tonight, I remind myself. Still, the team is trotting at an impressive pace, every tugline is tight and motionless and the empty sled skips and skids on hard-packed snow and patches of bare ice. By lining up the prominent rampart of Sentinel Point to the west with the crest of the barren hills northeast of the bay, I can tell that we are not yet halfway home. I briefly consider looking at my watch, buried on my wrist beneath five layers of cuffs, gloves and mitts. The thought passes: they're rolling right along. That's all I need to know.

The moon sets in a long arc. There are the sounds of sled runners bouncing on snow, eight dogs panting and the steady whisper of the wind. I can see the trail ahead of the dogs now. Evidently, the blow did not erase it so completely out here on the center of the bay. I glance back and signal to Mike again. His light comes back strong and steady, no closer than before. I call softly to my leaders, "Good boy, Beav, good dog, Troubles."

My thoughts wander back over the autumn. It has been a long season. At times it has felt as though our efforts with the dogs and the homestead were all a part of some giant board game—roll the dice, move back three squares, roll again, miss two turns . . . There have been trails to clear and reroute, with axes and balky, cold-blooded chainsaws.

There has been an ongoing battle to put an old snowmobile to work for us, an effort not aided by my mechanical ineptitude. There has been an endless round of dog chores, topped off by the sharing of our cramped little cabin with three newborn pups and an ailing, incontinent brood bitch. There has been the pervasive force of the subarctic's oncoming darkness and cold, and the seemingly endless wait for the windswept expanse of McLeod Bay to freeze.

Through it all, there has been our ongoing effort to bring these dogs into top athletic form. We teach them and test them. We feed and water them. We develop the habits of running and resting and the responses that will be vital to our success in the racing season ahead.

It is not easy, this life of a long-distance dog musher. Stripped of its romanticism and its magical, effortless moments—moments which are provided in abundance—it is an odd potpourri. It is a life of anyone keeping working animals, like that of a horseman with his stock. There are daily chores, the breeding and acquiring of new animals, the watchfulness for signs of sickness or injury. This is combined with many aspects of athletic life: training, nutrition, sponsorship, equipment and competition.

Through these, for most long-distance teams, is woven a life of wilderness subsistence—hauling firewood, hunting and fishing, gathering, gardening and building and living somewhere on the northern edge of civilization. Mixed with all of these, for all but the few full-time sled dog breeders and trainers, is seasonal work in some field more predictable and financially dependable than dog mushing. It is a demanding, many-layered life.

I do not say this in an effort to impress. This life that I and others have chosen is no harder, no more demanding of skill and ingenuity and perseverance, than the daily work and routines I know my more urban friends face. We choose our own reality, our own path, each one of us. Or by default we follow a path set out before us. I have chosen this life. It is a rich and good one.

I am tired and a little cold and a bit melancholy this Christmas night, yes. But I would not, in the dark and behind my team, trade places with anyone now struggling to merge into a lane choked with traffic on some holiday expressway. We are here. That other person is there. I live, we live, the way we do. Here in the North

COLD NIGHTS, FAST TRAILS

or there in the metropolis, we are lucky, yes and unlucky too, sometimes.

The horses smell the barn now. Ahead looms the bulk of a small granite island. We will swing behind it, cut west across the mouth of the Hoarfrost River and climb slightly off the lake ice into the yard of the homestead. For this final mile, I like to train my team to accelerate. Tonight they seem eager to do so without any encouragement from me, but I give them a high-pitched "Yip!" just for consistency. All eight of them break immediately from a trot into an effortless lope. They are oblivious to my weight, which is over 200 pounds, and to the weight of the big sled itself.

I don't know what can compare to the exhilaration of swift silent travel behind a team of sled dogs. Tonight feels like the final step of a long and arduous process of preparation. The dogs' paws skim the snow as we sail along. They exude strength and happiness with every puff of breath. If this team is not ready to race, I think smugly, I have never driven one that was.

The markers we have set out alongside our makeshift runway zip past in the dark. They are scraggly little spruce trees, alternating with others less rustic but more visible—black plastic sacks filled with snow. I think briefly ahead to tomorrow's flight out, the excitement of a large aircraft landing at the homestead and the uncertainty of our long drive south.

A fork in the trail pulls me back to the here and now. "Gee, Beaver, Gee!" I shout and Beaver cuts to the right with a flourish. The team slows a little as we climb off the lake and comes to a stop with a solid jerk, as I plant my heavy steel snowhook in the hardpack beside the cabin.

"Good dogs. You guys are good dogs," I tell them. I can see Mike's headlamp, as his team rounds the turn behind the island and starts down the runway. They are in the home stretch gallop, too. I am thrilled by the speed of his approaching light.

My dogs are standing in harness, breathing hard but still full of energy and enthusiasm. A team of huskies is always a beautiful sight to a musher. They look especially striking after a brisk run. Their bodies are tense and hardened, with frost rime all over their muzzles and necks. Their eyes are bright in the glare of the headlamp I have just turned on. I walk up and down the line, talking softly and clapping my hands, playing with them.

Eight dogs, each different from every other. In wheel position, closest to the sled, stand McLeod and Brew. McLeod is easily the most physically striking dog in the team. Jet black with piercing ice-blue eyes, he balances his intimidating size and strength with what Mike calls "the demeanor of a saint." Brew is all grizzled veteran by comparison—a no-nonsense, awkward-looking male, yet with a gait so surprisingly smooth he could balance a glass of champagne on his hips.

The next dogs up the gangline, in swing, are Nacho and Grayling. They, too, are a duet of veteran and rookie. Nacho is Brew's son and has inherited his silken trot but unfortunately not his tough black footpads. Grayling has twice finished the Iditarod Race for me, though his pedigree is full of galloping flat-out sprint dogs. Grayling had to *learn* to trot over the course of several years and he finally has the technique down pat.

In point, just back from the leaders, are Mist and Fuji. These two—Mist is white and Fuji is fox-red—are all daintiness and femininity, with a tiny dash of coy mischief thrown in. They are the "small" dogs that old-timers ask about when they see a modern dogteam. "Are those pups?" they wonder. No, I say again and again, they're both full-grown: Mist is three and Fuji four. Together they do not weigh over 80 pounds, I'm sure. They are both the kind of dogs that are nearly invisible in a big team, not because they are so small, but because they are always just *there*—pulling and running and never getting tangled, mile after mile after mile. Except, of course, when they come into heat.

7

In lead, as always for the past four years, is Beaver. Tonight he is teamed up with young Troubles, a perky, black-and-white adolescent with an insatiable attitude. He has a nimble gait and a fitting name. Beaver is fully in command. Troubles is just up there for a little education. Never fast, but always willing, Beaver has both limited and enhanced my team's efforts over the past three seasons. He is a nondescript, old brown-plug of a dog. He has never, not once, been dropped from a race. This year, though, may be his last season of racing. He is beginning to slow down, to choose his own speed as it suits him. He appears to tire when pushed from behind by a long string of eager young dogs. Still, when the wind blows the trail away and getting home is more important than getting home fast, Beaver proves his continued worth.

I walk back and forth, playing with this motley crew. At the end of a run is the moment when we are most in tune with each other. If there is ever a need to enforce discipline along the trail, it is done then and there with a swift cuff on the muzzle from my mittened hand, but it is now that I try to get back on good terms with every dog in the team. Patting and praising and roughing up their thick fur, I make sure no one is holding any grudges.

I step quickly inside the cabin and open the damper on the big barrel stove. Three eight-week-old white pups dash out the door and cause a mild ruckus amongst the team. A few of their puddles on the floor are quickly mopped up; we got off easy this time. I switch on the small 12-volt fluorescent light in the cabin and marvel again at such luxury after many winters of gas and kerosene lamps.

Mike's team has pulled in behind my sled and 16 dogs stand and stare at us as we talk.

"How was your run?"

"Pretty good. They were cooking right along."

"Mine too. Kind of nasty out there past the narrows, eh?"

"Yeah, it sort of surprised me."

"So McDougal strung them right out?"

"Yeah, no problem."

Mike and I have had a long autumn together, in solitude except for each other. Our conversations these days are lean, not unfriendly but certainly not effusive. We are both feeling our distance from our families this Christmas. We are eager for the next stage of the season to begin.

"Well, I'll water these guys and we can let them sit here awhile. Then I think I'll feed them right in harness before we put them away."

"Sounds good."

Every move we make with the team lately reflects our concentration on the coming races. In a race the team will pull into a checkpoint and pause, be watered and fed and move off to rest or to continue running. Thus, after each training run, we pause in front of the cabin, where the dogs relax for a few minutes before moving the last 200 feet to the dog yard.

I move down the line with a stack of battered bowls and one is tossed on the snow in front of each dog. Mike comes behind me with a pail of whitefish broth he boiled up in the afternoon. Each dog gets about a pint of the stew. Some of them drink eagerly, a few tip their bowls and nibble the chunks of fish off the snow and a few others move disdainfully away from the whole entree.

"Nacho, you sure are a fussy sonofabitch."

Nacho looks at me.

"But you're a good dog, Nach. Macho Nacho."

Still eyeing me, Nacho doesn't intervene as his partner Grayling eases his nose into his bowl and steals the chunks of fish from it.

"Go ahead, let Gray-dog eat your appetizer."

Mike has put a small kettle on the gas stove in the cabin. I go in and one by one the dogs sit or lie down, still in harness. We wait in silence for the water to boil and when it does we each pour off a cup and stir in a stiff helping of cocoa mix.

"Well, I hope we can keep these guys together for another couple of weeks," I offer.

"Yeah, with the road trip, you never know . . . and the temps."

"That's the biggest thing. If it's cold they'll be fine. If it's warm down there we'll be hurtin'. Plus we have to keep up with the vitamins and electrolytes and keep them clear of other dogs until we hit Duluth. And start easing them into some beaver meat, lamb. Stuff like that . . ."

Mike nods vacantly. He is hearing this whole worrisome monologue of mine for the umpteenth time.

Certainly all this fuss over the feeding, training and fastidious care of tough working huskies raises a few eyebrows amongst tried and true northerners. The image of sled dogs, and of dog driving in general, is founded upon the bygone days of 90-pound malamutes plodding before enormous sleighs, urged on by the snap and sting of the whip and the constant cursing of the drivers. These are all vivid and historically accurate images. But like all human endeavors, the working of dogteams has always been and will always be refined and altered to reflect new circumstances. Gone are the days when I can shoot a hundred caribou in the fall to feed six or seven dogs all winter. Gone too is the era when a 90-pound dog could earn its keep in a top-notch dogteam.

Lean, small-statured dogs are the norm these days and their relationship to their mushers has also evolved. Now the best dog mushers in the world are those who understand every aspect of their dogteams, from nutrition to psychology, to physical capability and athletic training techniques. The age-old pact between dogs and driver is still at the heart of the matter, but it is not tinged by the flagrant cruelty and off-season neglect that it once was. My concerns tonight about the impending stresses of travel and change are just the end result of this modern outlook. We are dog mushers, circa 1988.

A "musher"—one who mushes—is a term that comes from those days of big dogs, big loads, the whip and the struggle for survival. It comes from the French-Canadian and Métis dog drivers, who would tell their dogs, in no uncertain terms, to *"Marche! Marche!"* and, by all accounts, would then string on a list of elaborate descriptive names for the benefit of any dogs in the team who did not quite catch the meaning. *"Marche!"*, which loosely translates as "Get up!", became "Mush!" in Yankee slang and dog drivers became "mushers."

The word persists, as I hope it always does, although I have never heard a musher say "Mush!" to start his or her team moving. In spite of all that has changed, dog mushing retains its unmistakable aura of the past, of hard lives in hard lands and of romance. This aura is a part of the life for me, though perhaps some mushers would claim to have outgrown it.

I scoop the last bit of chocolate out of my cup and lick the spoon.

"Well, I'm gonna go feed these guys and put them away. Can you come out in a minute and run your team into the yard?"

The daily round of chores now comes full circle. In the morning, it is the scooping and hauling away of dog droppings and every evening, all year long, it is feeding time. Tonight the dogs spring to their feet as I tug the big plastic tub of food out the door of the cabin and stir it with an old shovel handle.

The food is a warm mush of dry dog food of the highest quality, soaked with gallons of warm water and mixed with some melted lard and scraps of meat. It is a standing joke among mushers that our dogs eat better than we do. I'm sure none of us are quite certain whether it is a joke after all. I do know that on nights when I am hungry after a long day in the cold, the dogs' rich stew smells delicious.

There is bedlam in the front yard for a few minutes, as I move down the two teams, plopping a steaming scoopful of dinner in front of each dog. Moments later there is only the sound of bowls being licked clean and some short growls over the final few tidbits.

Mike comes out and we each run our teams into the dog yard. This is a wide area of packed snow furnished with snug wooden houses. Stubby spruce poles are anchored firmly in the sand and snow alongside each doghouse and around them are looped long chains with brass snaps at their ends.

Mike and I tussle and joke with the dogs as we take them from their harnesses. They are playful and happy tonight. It is strange to have the dog yard empty except for these dogs, our "first string." All of the pups, yearlings and retirees have already moved down to Reliance, where one of the station weathermen will be taking care of them while we are "out."

Soon both teams are put away. Some of the dogs curl up in their houses; others frisk with their neighbors or stand and watch us. Mike hands me a bundle of harnesses and I turn to hang them on the long rope alongside the outbound trail.

"You may as well put those down with the other stuff, okay?"

I had forgotten about our departure tomorrow. "Yeah. Right." He smiles and I shake my head. "Hey— I knew that. I *knew* that."

We each pull a sled through the dog yard and down onto the lake. There, there is a mound of packs, boxes and dog food bags all stacked in preparation for the morning. Mike turns and heads back toward the house.

The stars are bright now. There is a new light falling softly on the homestead—the green ethereal light of the aurora borealis. I push back the frosted wolverine ruff of my parka and gaze upward. A shimmering curtain of green with a faint purple border undulates in a wide arc across the backdrop of stars. These "northern" lights are actually in the southern quadrant of the sky, for at this latitude they can appear anywhere.

I stand there looking at the lights for only a moment. Good flying weather tomorrow, I think as I turn up the trail to the cabin. The thermometer by the window reads −36 degrees.

My thoughts run ahead again, to the flight, the drive, the familiar trail of the Beargrease Race, the friends along the way. . . .

They are all a part of this dog mushing life, but the essence of it is all right here, on the shore of Great Slave Lake this Christmas night.

THE BREED

"**Y**ou FIGURE THAT SUSIE OF YOURS MIGHT THROW some good pups if she was bred back to her father? Try to get more of those tough feet with maybe a little less hound in there?"

"I dunno. I should think about doing that, though. She just had pups by Tanner, so I think I'll wait 'til next spring before breeding her again. . . ."

"Yeah, I suppose you need her now. . . . Well, I heard from Jeff in Fairbanks the other day. Sounds like they've got good snow already."

"Yeah? Did he say anything about the purse for the Yukon Quest?"

"Nope and I forgot to ask him. You think it'll go up?"

"You *forgot* to ask him? You need to get your mind more on money, chum! Are you a dog musher or just another dilettante? Call him up again and find out!"

We laugh. It is a warm day in October in northern Minnesota—too warm for the two of us, with teams of dogs to train and the first race of the winter less than three months away. On a day like this, though, it's hard

15

to feel too impatient with the weather. The sunlight has that clarity and sharpness that comes only in autumn, the relative humidity is down near zero and the air feels fresh and clean on my skin. I am sitting cross-legged on the hood of my old truck, talking with a friend who has just sold me a dog. I'm "leaving any minute," as I have been for the past hour. It will be dark by the time I get home, no matter when I leave, so I see no reason to rush.

Dog mushers, though sometimes portrayed as taciturn and even a bit simple, love to talk. Each of us has a circle of confidantes with whom we share plans and stories and aspirations that we hesitate to tell others. These friends are our sounding boards; we bounce ideas off them just to see how they sound out loud. We might see these cohorts only once every few months, maybe only once in a year, but the connection is there and the bond is strong. They understand. In any pursuit as far removed from the mainstream of modern life as dog mushing, that understanding, that set of premises and assumptions about what is and what is not important, is treasured. We crave the opportunity to talk dogs, talk racing, talk strategy and contenders and breeding and sled designs. Like fanatics in every pursuit from stock cars to mountaineering, we are happiest when we are doing either one of two things—pursuing our passion, or talking about it with those who share it.

Dog mushers are a breed, with as many different strains and variations as any breed. And the dogs that bring us together, whom we discuss in such careful detail on warm October afternoons, are also a breed. In trying to convey some of the feeling and some of the lore of long-distance dog mushing, it is vital to begin with a discussion of the breeds, both canine and human.

One question I have often been asked by spectators at races, gas-pump attendants along northern highways and friends unfamiliar with sled-dog racing is "What breed are your dogs?" I think these people hope I will say, "Siberian" or "Samoyed" or "Malamute"—all recognized kennel club categories. To this, they could nod approvingly and tell me that their neighbor, or daughter, or whoever, has a nice big malamute and "it's just the most beautiful dog you'd ever want to see." However, the conversation doesn't follow that script very often in modern dog mushing. To the question, "What breed are your dogs?" comes the thoughtful, drawn-out "Well . . . ." as the musher collects his or her thoughts and decides how to answer it, this time.

Sled dogs, by definition, pull sleds. Irish setters are sled dogs when they pull sleds, just as they are retrievers when they retrieve birds or watchdogs when they bark at the people who just pulled into the driveway. "Sled dog" does not describe a particular breed of dog any more than "draft horse" describes a specific breed of horse. In a dog world concerned with show standards, purebreds and pedigrees, the admission by a dog musher that his or her dogs are "a little bit of a lot of different breeds" is taken by many curious onlookers as an admission of a major fault, almost the confession of a petty crime. Most people *know* that the best dogs are purebred. After all, they say, aren't those the ones that sell for the high prices?

16,000 dollars sounds like a lot of money. Having never been near a dog show or a kennel club meeting, I cannot say with certainty that this sum is the most money ever paid for a single dog. Yet this is rumored to be the final price of a sled dog sold recently to some European buyers by an Alaskan musher. Was this dog purebred? Not by a long way, at least not in the usual understanding of that term. This was simply a dog that seemed to be "prepotent," to use the breeders' term, for siring top-notch offspring. In this case, the parameters of top-notch are not at all related to color of coat, color of eyes, or show-room obedience. This dog's attributes and those he had proven he could pass on to his offspring can be summed up in four words—tough, fast, eager and re-sponsive—at about $4,000 for each word. He is, in the estimation of his seller and, obviously, his buyers, a paragon of sled dog performance and breeding potential.

Most dogs that run in long-distance teams, pulling sleds, share many traits that help them resemble the popular image of a sled dog—a long wolfish muzzle, pointed ears, a thick coat, a curled tail, well-furred feet with tough pads. Yet as I write that sentence, a parade of dogs comes to mind, good sled dogs from good teams, with Irish-setter faces, floppy ears, thin greyhound coats, straight rat tails and tender feet. Here again, the traditional romantic view is challenged and those holding it are dismayed. Surely, the diehards think, in the world of the North, the struggle for survival, these scrawny crossbred speedsters can never truly measure up. I once cherished that same opinion, as do many starry-eyed beginning mushers.

Sled dogs are dogs that pull sleds. Period. Long-distance sled dogs are those that pull sleds hundreds, even thousands of miles in a single expedition, or race, or tour of the neighborhood. To genetically categorize the top dogs from this field of amazing animals would be the work of many years. By the time the task was completed it would already be outdated.

Tough, fast, eager and responsive dogs are bred to other dogs that the breeder feels will complement and reinforce those desirable characteristics. By some, this is done with all the finesse and knowledge that comes from a thorough understanding of genetics and heredity. For others, breeding is dictated by the simple maxim: "Breed outstanding dogs to outstanding dogs . . . only and always." Both approaches have improved sled dog traits and performance over many years and this process will continue as long as there are dog teams in the world.

To those who think this sounds too scientific, too heartless and detached, I can only say, "Watch the dogs." Watch how carefully they are raised and trained and conditioned. Watch how their performance continues to topple old records and make treks that years ago would have been considered impossible. Watch them at the finish line of the Iditarod Trail Race, coming into Nome, Alaska, at a steady swift trot in the teams of Susan Butcher, Rick Swenson, Joe Runyan and many others— 1,100 miles behind them in just over 11 days. These dogs, these "mongrels" of the north, are athletes and workers without equal in the animal world. And through all of this, these dogs have about them an unmistakable happiness.

This stems from the fact that they are performing the work for which their instincts and physical traits are completely adapted. All of the cross-breeding and intermixing of incongruous bloodlines notwithstanding and with the exception of a few rare teams, modern sled dogs have all come from ancient arctic roots. If one follows the many long lines back through the pedigrees of these dogs, one eventually finds them all to have at least some percentage of "husky." Husky is used here as a generic term, denoting the origins of dogs trained to pull sleds by the original people of Siberia, North America and Greenland.

Over the course of hundreds and thousands of years, these native northern working dogs have been very selectively bred, whether or not their owners were conscious of that process. The toughest, strongest, smartest and fastest dogs were the dogs that *survived*. They survived starvation, summertime neglect, life-and-death struggles with their kin and winter journeys through some of the most hostile weather and terrain in the world. At various times, by human intent or by accident, they may have bred back to the wolves of the north and reacquired some of those quirks and strengths and adaptations.

Modern sled dog driving and racing began most conspicuously in the goldfields of Nome at the turn of the century. At that time the breeding of dogs began to be influenced by conscious long-range planning and scientific understanding. The basic stock that was the starting point was already remarkably well-adapted to the task at hand. The husky of the North, whether Siberian, Alaskan, Greenlandic or Canadian, was a dog bred for performance. This is still the case and all of the cross-breeding over the years has only been aimed at improvement of this amazingly sound stock with some specific attribute of sled-dog performance—all-out speed, improved responsiveness, a faster trot or such esoteric attributes as a better appetite under stress.

I have run sled dogs whose ancestry goes back to such diverse breeds as setter, dingo, saluki and Siberian husky. Finally, after ten years of running and training and breeding sled dogs, I am beginning to know what I want. Some other mushers progressed much faster in their learning. After only a few seasons, they set out to breed, train and field a superlative team.

This quest is a long process. One cannot predictably stamp out new dogs from improved molds, day after day. Our teams and kennels are governed by all the mystery, unpredictability and beauty of life. There are inalterable rules involved—the rules of genetics, life span, nutrition, anatomy and psychology. There is also the element of chance, or luck, or "random selection"—the uncertainty that every musher and breeder faces.

Breeding, racing and traveling with sled dogs, even simply owning 8 or 20 or 50 dogs—not one of these endeavours makes any "sense." In a world that claims to reward only those who streamline their lives, cut away physical labor and strive to reduce their direct contacts with the natural world, dog mushers are understandably viewed as "a little odd" at best and "crazy" more often. I agree wholeheartedly with this assessment. If the world of music videos, stock portfolios and suburbia is sane, we mushers are all certifiably "bonkers." But who are we and why do we drive dogs?

In turning from the dogs to an overview of the people who keep and mush teams of them, any yearning for accurate generalizations will once again be frustrated.

Dog mushers are as diverse as the dogs to whom they devote themselves. At one time, they were all people whose lives were inextricably tied to the wilderness and to winter. They were hunters and gatherers, trappers, prospectors, couriers, traders and freight haulers. Today sled dog kennels thrive in the most remote corners of the Far North, as well as in proximity to large cities and in climates a thousand miles from the Arctic or sub-Arctic.

Along with the modern era of dog mushing have come dog food technology and marketing that free the musher from a wilderness food supply. Staple sled dog rations now come more frequently from 50-pound labeled sacks than from the fish nets, traps and hunting efforts of the mushers. Thus, given enough money, there are no longer any *de facto* limits on the geographical range of sled dog teams, on the numbers of dogs in kennels, or on the type of work the musher does apart from his or her team of dogs.

There are lawyers who are well-known and successful mushers, training and traveling on the same trails as trappers, gold miners, dentists and construction workers. But there is still a "breed" of person here, quite apart from that person's profession, their place of residence or the size of their dog lot.

Dog mushers are hard drivers. By that I mean that they set goals for themselves and their teams and push hard to achieve them. They are risk takers. Anyone with any knowledge of the uncertainties involved with travel by dogteam would agree to that. They are workers, in the old-fashioned sense of physical, dirty and, at times, unpleasant labor. They clean kennels. They haul firewood. They butcher animals. They lug pails of feed and water, day after day, year after year.

Dog mushers are innovators. They constantly seek to streamline the process of keeping, training and, of course, running their dogs, be it with a new sled design, a different length or type of gangline, an untested cloth

21

for dog booties, a radically different training regimen, or a brighter headlamp bulb.

Dog mushers are, or quickly learn to be, thrifty. So high are the costs of fielding a competitive team and so limited the resources of most teams in terms of sponsorship and actual profit from the races, that penny-pinching becomes second nature to all mushers after a few seasons. This is almost as true of the mushers who are lawyers and surgeons as it is of the trappers and salmon fishermen. Until dog mushing hits the big time, it is likely that the majority of mushers will continue to lurch around the continent in tired, old pickup trucks, packed to overflowing with gear and dogs.

Dog mushers are people who are unmistakably *native northerners* in their outlook. I mean this with no racial reference and with no regard for birthplace. They have chosen dog mushing despite many "sensible" alternatives—for instance, snowmobiles for back-country travel and skis for sport. They have decided that this pursuit, despite what anyone else thinks, makes sense for them and appeals to them at a deep level. It is the same kind of acknowledgment that every devoted northerner makes, in a culture so obsessed with the "desirable" climates of California, Arizona and Florida. It is a stubborn devotion to something truly and completely northern. Dog mushers enjoy the bond they keep with working animals and accept all that goes with it—sacrifice, expense, inconvenience, daily effort and a re-ordering of the priorities that society seeks to set for us all.

Dog mushers are the kind of people whom others refer to as "interesting," with a slight inflection that suggests this might be a euphemism for "peculiar." But whether they drive to work from the suburbs of Ottawa or trap marten in the foothills of the Alaska Range, dog mushers do not concern themselves very much with what other people think of them. After all, there are dogs to train, trails to work on, sleds to rebuild and pups to feed.

I remember one conversation with a friend of mine on a January night in northern Wisconsin. Kenny Jones is an energetic and masterful craftsman, a high school teacher and an aspiring dog musher. After he had warmed me up with a few beers, he turned to me with a philosophical look in his eyes and said, "You know, Dave, I've done a lot of things, learned a lot of skills. Canoe building, cabinet-making, welding, mechanical stuff . . ."

I nodded, envious of his success in these pursuits.

"But you know something? This dog mushing, this is *hard*. I mean, damn it, this is *difficult!*"

I nodded again. I knew exactly what he meant. Every dog musher does and few non-mushers ever will. And somewhere in that difficulty Kenny was facing, I suspect, is an important part of what keeps us all at it.

At some point, for every serious musher, the rewards of sled dog driving have gone beyond the massage of ego and the thrill of adventure and have touched a nerve. It is a timeless challenge and satisfaction, always uncertain, that makes the life worthwhile and that makes dog mushers, like their dogs, a distinct breed.

GREENHORN

O.K., CHEECHAKO, HERE'S WHAT YOU CAME for, I told myself. I was on Wagosh Lake, in Minnesota's Boundary Waters, on a snowy gray day in February, 1978. I was about to step onto the runners of a dogsled for the first time in my life. As "cheechako," a tenderfoot, a greenhorn, I was about to experience for the first time a way of travel that would eventually lead me far to the north, west nearly to Siberia, into debt up to my eyeballs more than once and through many sleepless nights on the trail and on the road. But first, of course, there had to be a photograph.

I still have that picture. I stand on the runners of the sled, a wool cap perched jauntily on my head, my skinny, pale, college-student forearms resting confidently on the handlebar, suspenders and a wool union suit giving me the look (I figured) of the old woodsman. The dogs, seven of them, are strung out in front of the sled, Turok and Mukluk in lead. Are they grinning in anticipation of what would happen next?

Pictures snapped, posterity satisfied, I shouted "O.K.!" about two seconds after the dogs had already nearly jerked me off the runners with a sudden, lunging start. The snowhook plowed and bounced through the drifts alongside the sled, clanging into the stanchions and throwing puffs of snow into the air as the team churned ahead.

"Pick up the hook!" Duncan shouted from alongside the trail. Right, pick up the hook—I feel like I'm on the back ladder of a runaway caboose. I leaned down and with my mittened hand caught the bouncing steel snowhook just as the lead dogs hit the start of the portage, made the sharp turn and planted novice musher, sled, snowhook and all deeply into a drift of shoreline snow. This could be trickier than it looks, I mumbled. All feeling quickly left my snow-covered forearms and an icy trickle of melting snow made its way down my oh-so-woodsy union suit.

Everyone long remembers their first impression of any powerful experience, and dog mushing, no matter what its purpose or accoutrements, is always an experience loaded with power. In my memory, the animals of that first team are larger than life. The sled was impossibly clumsy and unbalanced. The trail was filled with an endless procession of trees, rocks, tight turns and steep hills. I will never forget my first hour of dog mushing between Wagosh and Niki Lakes.

Nor will I ever forget the powerful impression that came to me that day, overshadowing my panic and injured pride—the impression that here was something that I would be doing a lot of in my life.

I cannot explain that premonition. I have never felt it again the way I did then. It was as if, when I first stepped up on the thick oak runners of that old freight sled and looked ahead at the dogs, I was looking down a long tunnel of years and miles, far into the future and far to the north.

It was an accurate hunch I had that day, but it held none of the details of the many moments, good and bad, thrilling and tedious, that eventually turn greenhorns into dog mushers. It is probably just as well. I know of few undertakings so filled with emotional and physical highs and lows as dog mushing. It is as if there is no middle ground in the realm of sled dog work. The going is smooth and fast, or exhausting and slow. The reality is, of course, that there is much in-between experience, but the good and bad times are so emotionally charged and memorable that they eclipse the humdrum, nondescript days and miles.

Dog mushing is a skill and a way of life, still passed from one person to the next almost entirely by apprenticeship. There are few "how-to" books in the field. There are so many different facets to be mastered, so many seemingly trivial but ultimately critical details to attend to, that one can learn only from those who have in turn learned from others. Probably there are people who have become good dog mushers without benefit of a mentor, but they must be rare indeed and persistent far beyond mere stubbornness.

That day along the Minnesota-Ontario border, I began to learn the techniques of working with a team of sled dogs. I spent my boyhood in the rolling dairy farm country of northern Illinois. I lived in a small town home far removed from fields, chores and animals and even farther away from sled dogs. As I grew older, I becamed obsessed with the world of the mountains, with rock climbing and backpacking and mountaineering. Later my attention focused more on the North, the Canadian "bush," with winter travel on skis and summer trips by canoe. Then, in 1978, I learned of an outdoor school and outfitting service begun by Duncan Storlie and Will Steger, called Lynx Track Winter Travel.

Lynx Track organized treks in northern Minnesota and taught the use of cross-country skis, dogteams, wall tents, snowshoes and all the traditional methods of winter life in the woods. I was determined to attend their program, so with money borrowed from home, I registered for their eight-day "advanced course"—a trip up through

COLD NIGHTS, FAST TRAILS

Cedar, Mudro, Gun and Wagosh Lakes. Our group of eight people, each of us on skis and carrying backpacks, traveled with seven dogs and a single huge sled. As I look back on that trip, I know that I was laughably self-conscious, eager and filled with preconceived notions gleaned from Robert Service doggerel and Jack London stories.

Duncan Storlie and Mitch Gilbert, our teachers on that trip, were for several years to be my mentors in the north woods. From them I began to learn the fine points of sled building, dog care, wood cutting, cabin construction, fish netting, hunting and on through the long list of activities that make up a northern backwoods life. They were both there that day on Wagosh Lake when Turok and Mukluk deposited me in the snowbank. They laughed at me then, but I knew that they were simply recalling many similar experiences of their own. Over the years that I worked with Duncan and Mitch, I gradually acknowledged the intricate complexity of the so-called simple life and I began to appreciate the rewards that came from mastering the endless details, one by one. They were good teachers, always ready with ridicule or hyperbole or assistance, whichever seemed appropriate.

As a beginner I had all the usual notions about what a sled dog was and wasn't. For a short time I had owned a 120-pound malamute named Bandit, more stubborn and thick-headed than any dog I've known since. Just as I was beginning to come to grips (quite literally) with him, he was poisoned in a freak accident. I was not to own a dog again for three years, though I worked with Duncan's team each winter as if it was my own.

We began training the dogs each November near Duncan's home in the far western suburbs of Minneapolis. Our training cart was a laughable little contraption with six-inch tires, a flimsy metal frame and no brakes except for the three or four old truck tires we would drag along behind us. On this rig, one of us would set off with a team of dogs down the Luce Line—an abandoned railroad grade running west out of the Twin Cities—where the ever-present hazards came mostly in the form of busy road crossings and wandering pets of every shape and size.

I remember one devastating run, my last on the Luce Line. It was a cloudy, cool November day, late in the afternoon, and rather than run twice with small teams, I decided to hook up all seven dogs, drag three tires and get finished before dark. Off we went down the pea gravel at an insane pace. As we neared the fifth road crossing, I spotted a farm dog tearing toward us across a horse pasture. We had never come this far before and we had never encountered this dog. As we reached the road, the farm dog, a collie, reached his owner's fence—three electrified strands of wire. He stopped there, yapping and leaping and taunting my team. It was too much for Turok. We swung down the paved road a short distance, then directly toward the collie, the electric fence and the pasture. I don't remember what I was saying as the team turned, but it would never be printed here.

I think my dogs went between the lowest and middle strands of wire. That was a solid fence, because it stopped the cart dead as we struck it at what seemed like a speed slightly below Mach 1. I don't remember feeling a jolt of current from the fence through the metal frame of the cart, but there must have been one. The team had the collie down on the ground, fur was flying, blood was flowing and I landed squarely in the midst of the brawl after being thrown forward over the wires.

Unfortunately, I am all too familiar with the scene that followed, because I have had to go through it several times over the years. The trick is to gradually pry each of the sled dogs away from the hapless pet and in the one split second when no one has a mouthful of collie or lab or poodle or whatever it is, give the poor critter a mighty heave that will land it out of reach of the team. Then gather in as many tuglines, collars, necklines and legs as you can and sit tight until the owner appears on the scene—usually a matter of seconds.

I arrived back at Storlie's house that evening encrusted with mud, horse manure, dog hair and three flavors of blood—collie, husky and greenhorn musher. I was certain I was bearing unheard-of tales and had been the victim of unprecedented bad luck. I pulled into the driveway, hobbled out of the truck's cab and was greeted by Duncan and Mitch in the garage that was our workshop. I launched into my story. They both stood there, calm and quiet, nodding their heads.

"Welcome to the club," said Mitch.

Duncan nodded, "Yeah. That happens. You get the guy's phone number? And are *you* O.K.?"

I was bitten in several places during the melee, but all the dogs, collie included, had had their rabies shots. Dunc paid the vet bill on the beat-up collie, it recovered quickly and the owner, an old farmer, was understanding about the whole affair. "That darn dog will chase anything," he said, "but this is a new one."

That night, as we went out to put the dogs back in their kennel, I knew that I did not want to keep sled dogs in the suburbs for too much longer.

Over the winters that followed I worked for Lynx Track and I became enough of a dog musher to appreciate that here was something that could take me a lifetime to learn. It seemed that the trips by dogteam that we made in those winters were all demanding, all fraught with unexpected weather—January thunderstorms, below-zero Aprils—and filled to the brim with the infamous law of Murphy. Lynx Track struggled financially through those years. Duncan's and Will's vision was a good one, but it was ten years ahead of its time. Cold, winter, sled dogs and wall tents were, in the 70s, still too far out on the edge of the typical wilderness enthusiast's imagination.

Our days and nights on the trail were filled with moments memorable for their beauty and for their misery. It felt as if we lived from November through April in overdrive. At first, I thought this was simply the normal growing period of any small business and I think my cohorts shared this view. But gradually, as the seasons passed, as endless "all-nighters" of packing out food, pine-tarring skis, loading sleds and repairing gear blurred together in my memory, I began to understand and grudgingly accept that this was not likely to change. Much as we assured each other that Fat City was just around the next bend in the trail, we were already there. We were at least as close as we were going to get.

Through it all, there were the dogs. They were the spark, the magic, in what was at times a tedious and laborious life. Whenever I stepped onto the back of a sled my sense of excitement and wonder returned, lifting my bedraggled outlook on many nights and mornings. I was steadily becoming aware, firsthand, of what these animals could do and of the depth and breadth of spirit they possessed.

I remember one night as a watershed of my involvement with Lynx Track. Late in the afternoon we had come in from an eight-day trip, back to the roadhead north of Ely, Minnesota, with a group of six people. After saying good-bye to them, I turned a small team back into the woods toward our tipi camp three miles down the trail. It was after ten.

There had been a very heavy snowfall while we had been out on our trip and the trail was unbroken. For some unavoidable reason that I have forgotten, the sled was loaded far too heavily. The four dogs in my team were tired after a full day of work; it was dark and cold. In those winters I never used a headlamp at night—I had simply not become familiar with them yet.

That three miles of plodding, with the huge sled tipping sideways every few yards, took me well over two hours. At one point I stopped, sweating, cursing and at the limit of my patience. I was wearing, by then, only a light shirt and it was soaked with sweat although the temperature was well below zero. I leaned back to rest a moment on top of that impossible load.

I must have slept, for I remember opening my eyes to the clear bright stars, a deep chill within me, my shirt and brow heavily crusted with ice. I stood, shivering violently and urged the dogs on, frightened by the realization of what I had just done, how tired I was, how dark and cold and hostile the night suddenly seemed. We arrived at the deserted camp at last. When Duncan found me, I was sitting in the wall tent, facing the Yukon stove, its last embers glowing, with my head tipped forward and my hands on my boot laces, sound asleep.

He woke me, we ate and talked of the course that would begin in the morning, of what must be done and which of us would do it. During the night Duncan became ill; he staggered out several times into the cold. Returning once, chilled and exhausted and nauseous, he spoke seriously and without his habitual irony or humor: "I'll remember this night when I'm trying to decide whether to do this next year."

Evidently, he remembered it well, because that was the final year of our work together at Lynx Track. I bought those dogs from Duncan the following winter and with that purchase my involvement with sled dogs deepened drastically. I owned a team. No longer would I be free from dogs at winter's end, to take up with them again in the fall. They were my dogs, my responsibilities, mine to train and feed and vaccinate and travel with.

I will never forget those seven dogs. One of them, Chiala, who was just a yearling then, is still with me. Popcorn, the patriarch of the team, is dead. Mukluk, Sinker and Ralph are still at work, now for the Outward Bound School in northern Minnesota. Turok and Bandit were sold to a trapper in the Northwest Territories, in order to raise enough money so that I could get home one spring.

As I've said, one must have a mentor in order to become a good dog musher. But within and alongside that process of learning from another musher, one learns directly from the dogs. They have traveled many more miles than the rookie musher, unless they too are just beginners. Even with a single experienced dog in the team, the driver has a good teacher from whom to learn the ropes. This may sound like a Walt Disney script, but I will stand by it. In the miles we share with our dogs, the evenings we feed them, the mornings we clean their yards and fill their water bowls, the times we together slog through slush, break through thin ice, or struggle with heavy loads in deep snow, the communication and "training" flow constantly in both directions.

Seasons and years pass and a musher realizes that he or she *knew* what that dog's next move would be in some ticklish situation, or *felt* in the dark the precise moment when the wheel dogs would slam into their tuglines to dislodge a heavy sled.

Strange things happen. On my first winter trip into Quetico Park in Ontario, I traveled with two friends. I was not guiding the trip and thus it was a pleasant change for me in the midst of my winter work. The dogs I had then were not yet formally mine, but we had begun to be aware of each other, to tolerate weakness and appreciate strength, in the way that mushers and their own teams do.

Leaving McIntyre Lake early one day, my two companions started out ahead on skis. The dogs and I were to follow them after I finished packing up our camp. Everything went smoothly, the dogs started off in a strong and happy rush and I was proud of them and of myself with them. My pride was of the self-indulgent sort that so often foreshadows disaster. That morning as we crossed the portage into Sarah Lake, the dogs were racing headlong down the trail with a top-heavy, awkward sled. As a musher, at that moment, I was beyond my limits, but I would not admit it. I had learned no tricks for such situations yet, like removing the dogs' tuglines and letting them run only on necklines, or wrapping a chain or rope completely around the sled runners to provide extra drag.

Faster and faster we sped along, until with a decisive crunch the sled slammed squarely into the trunk of a huge red pine, stopping instantly. But the team did not stop. In some transfer of the momentum of the sled to the forward motion of the dogs—a physicist could diagram it—the stout steel eyebolt at the front of the sled was bent open, the bridle rope broke and the team ran on, flat out and gaining speed, down the portage.

I called to them as mushers always do to runaway teams—begging, pleading, cursing, commanding—but I knew full well that they were not about to stop for a minor matter like a lost sled. I tugged the sled back onto the trail, maneuvered it down to the ice of Sarah Lake and put on my skis. Then I realized what could happen. A trail we had made two days before led east to Kashahpiwi Lake and north from there. That was where the dogs had gone the last time we had come through Sarah Lake, but today Kurt and John were going to turn south, off that trail, into Tuck Lake. I hoped that they hadn't reached the turnoff yet. If they were still on this old stretch of trail, they would be able to tackle the team as it came up on them from behind. They would realize what had happened and bring the dogs back to the sled.

But they had already turned. Two pairs of ski tracks veered south and the tracks of the seven dogs went straight east. I skied after the team. I crossed more portages, miles passed and I was nearly to Kashahpiwi.

Usually when a team gets away, it carries the sled with it. Eventually the sled tips over, tangles in brush, or collides with a tree. The team stops. That day, there was no sled to tip or tangle or crash. I wondered where I would eventually find those dogs.

Suddenly, there they were. Not stopped ahead resting, not tangled and fighting, but heading straight toward me, tongues out, paws skimming the trail, an unmistakable twinkle in their eyes.

In this situation, a musher, especially a green musher like me, is filled with two opposing urges—one to beat the lead dogs to within an inch of their lives and the other to welcome the team back and assure everyone that you are very glad to see them, which you are. That day I did both, but I have since decided that the friendly approach is the most sensible. Now whenever I recover a runaway team, I pat them and tussle happily with them, meanwhile calling them every name in the book in an effort to vent my own frustration.

We turned back down the trail and I had a harrowing ride as I skijored behind seven strong dogs. By the time we arrived back at the sled, icicles streamed back from the sides of my eyes, caused by the cold wind and my wide-eyed effort to keep upright and not lose the team again. I hitched the dogs to the sled and quickly caught up with John and Kurt. I will never know how far that team traveled, why they finally turned back, or how they managed to do so without becoming tangled.

Unlike the majority of modern dog mushers, who are involved in competition, I did not at first have a large network of fellow enthusiasts with whom I could exchange information, innovation and dog talk. Our winter guiding and spring travels in the far north were a world apart from the circles of competitive teams. We used the basic equipment that we had used from the start, changing and improving it very slowly over the years. Our dogs were simply what we called "good dogs"—large, strong, friendly, slow and always willing. In those days I would not have considered buying, selling, leasing or trading dogs as racers often do in their efforts to assemble championship teams. In fact, during those years, I never passed up an opportunity to berate the competitive side of dog mushing. Those formative seasons in my own career as a musher were somewhat stunted—I was enamored of some techniques and premises that it would take me a long time to outgrow and leave behind.

Gradually, I came to believe that I was no longer a greenhorn. I knew my business, my equipment and my dogs. I had cared for a team year-round, raised and trained some pups and built sleds from scratch. Within the limits of what we were doing there in Minnesota, I had progressed from tenderfoot to veteran in four or five seasons. But that was a tiny segment of the dog mushing world and our techniques and standards were crude and outmoded in comparison to advancements being made elsewhere.

In January of 1982 I entered my fastest three dogs in the three-dog race in Ely, Minnesota. We came to the race towing an open box trailer with the dogs chained inside. In the parking area filled with fancy kennel trucks from all over North America, we stood out like a kid in high-top sneakers and cut-off blue jeans at the starting line of a marathon. The racing began and we carefully proceeded to the starting chute at our assigned time. The dogs were Sinker, Ralph and Mukluk and their combined weight must have been well over 200 pounds. They pulled me on the lightest freight toboggan I had been able to scrounge from the workshop out at Lynx Track. We were ready to turn the dog racing world on its ear.

The course was three miles long and we covered it in a little over 15 minutes—a blistering 12 miles an hour. The winning team's time was around the ten-minute mark, maybe even less. Thirty-five teams had run the race that day. We finished 35th. The dog racing world didn't bat an eye.

I was a greenhorn all over again when I made two springtime expeditions by dogteam up the coast of Hudson Bay and out onto the barrenlands east of Great Slave Lake. Slowly I comprehended the narrow limits of my dog mushing experience. As with my first treks by dogteam in Minnesota, I went through the pride-wrenching process of seeing "proven" equipment fail, "good" dogs falter and "realistic" goals become impossible dreams. We were still paying our dues, my dogs and companions and I, and in hindsight our many mistakes are all too obvious.

In late October of 1980, I had traveled over to Grand Marais, Minnesota, to look at some dogs that Arleigh Jorgenson thought he might sell to my partners and me for use on a trip in the Arctic the following spring. That muddy, rainy afternoon was a staggering experience for me. I had never been to the kennel of a serious sled dog racer and breeder. Everywhere I looked there were dogs. They were, to my eye, all scrawny, skittish and unsuitable for the trip we were planning.

We hitched 12 of them to a huge truck-chassis training rig and three of us climbed aboard to go for a test drive. Each of us weighed at least 180 pounds, the chassis looked like it weighed a ton and those dogs flew out of the yard so fast that we nearly skidded out of control on the first three corners. These were dogs that Arleigh thought could help us out. They could not quite make his competitive team. He was willing to lend them, sell them, or have us use them and try to sell them up north. Foolishly, we declined all his offers. That spring we often had time to reflect on our decision, as we plodded across the tundra behind two very overworked five-dog teams.

That visit opened my eyes to a different dimension of dog mushing, but at the time I did not like what I saw. I assumed that any semblance of knowing each dog was impossible in a yard of 50 or more. As I tallied up the feed and expenses that went into a kennel of that size, I vowed that I would never pursue that course with my own brand of dog mushing.

At that time a 50-pound sack of Brand-X dog food, combined with scraps from whitefish netting and a box of fat trimmings from the local butcher, would feed my team for a full three weeks. Arleigh went through a bag of high-octane dog food every single day. My mind boggled. "Never," I remember saying to my friends as we drove away, "never." Six years later I owned 44 dogs.

Slowly, sometimes painfully, a musher's horizons widen—beyond the first few dogs, beyond local trails or traplines, past those first tentative races or expeditions or work projects. Gradually we learn that there are some very smart people in this business, doing some very clever things. Tim White and his high-tech toboggan sleds, George Attla with his training and racing success, the Redington family and their successful breeding efforts and huge dog lots. Seeing these professionals, every musher faces a decision as to the place that dogs and mushing are to occupy in his or her own life. Everyone finds their own level of involvement, their own satisfactions and sacrifices.

For me, the first thoughts toward "turning professional" with my dogs came about six years ago. To me, "professional" meant that I would begin a process of education—learning all I could, subscribing to the small periodicals concerned with sled dogs, talking to the experts when I had a chance and pursuing new ideas and standards in the care and nutrition of my team. In effect, I decided to become a greenhorn again. I wanted to learn skills not only from a few close friends who were part-time mushers, but from the people who had completely devoted years of their lives to sled dogs.

I decided then that long-distance racing was the best proving ground for the kinds of dogs and mushing that appealed to me. By training for and competing in long-distance events, I could still keep a team versatile enough for work projects, occasional guiding and long noncompetitive expeditions. I was tired, at that time, of teaching "Sled Dogs 101" to beginners, week after week all winter long. I was restless and ready to adopt the single-minded devotion to a top-notch team of dogs that racing demands. I decided to ignore my doubts and jump into long-distance dog mushing with both feet.

It was a decision that would ultimately separate me from those "few good dogs" who had taught me so much. The core of my first team continues to work at the Outward Bound School in Minnesota, doing the courses for which they are perfectly suited. Today, as I look out from my cabin to the dogyard, I see only one member of my first dogteam. Chiala is old, now spayed and slightly overweight. She cannot keep up with the team I drive now, but I will keep her until the day she dies. She is a reminder to me of where my dogs and I have been and of where we are trying to go.

PUPS

SOUND ASLEEP. THEY LIE IN THE CORNER OF THEIR plywood house, a jumble of furry blonde and gray puppies. They spend at least nine-tenths of their time sleeping; during the moments they are awake, they eat. Gaining weight at a rate of seven percent per day is a full-time job—imagine a 20-pound child gaining ten pounds in a week. No wonder they're so tired!

I step into the pen; Rajah gives a quick alarm bark and backs toward the corner to defend her piled-up brood. "It's okay, girl; just me," I tell her. But she is not persuaded. A low growl rumbles in her throat. I can see I will get nowhere with her around. "Okay, Grouchy, come with me." I ease my hand to her collar and she grudgingly submits as I lead her out to an empty spot in the dog yard and clip her to a chain. She is calm as I walk back to the pen. Despite her instinctive grumbling, she is now accustomed to these times of separation from her puppies. She seems to enjoy the respites from the demanding work of nursing and mothering.

"Pupupupupup!" I call out in a high falsetto. The squirming pile wriggles further into the corner of the carpeted brood house. "Hey, you little rug rats, it's time to get weighed." They sleep. I set up the little scale on an overturned water dish and put the notebook down on the sawdust that covers the floor of the pen.

These pups are four weeks old today. Already I have seen several of them eating solid food from their mother's dish and clumsily stomping around their small square world. Their eyes have been open for nearly three weeks, but they still have the unnerving blank stare of all infants. I reach into the mound of furry bodies and lift one out, the only male of this litter; he squeals and wriggles furiously in my grip for a moment. I stroke his ample double chins and look him over briefly. He is plump—no better word can be found for pups of this age. The tiny scab at his navel is flaking away now. So are the small sores that had formed on the backs of his rear paws as he scrambled for traction on the plywood during his first frantic efforts to reach Rajah's teats.

Into a cardboard box he goes, atop the scale. He weighs in at 6¾ pounds, up from 4½ exactly one week ago. Already the litter has been given a dose of worming medicine, to combat the ubiquitous roundworms of young dogs. At six weeks, they will receive their first vaccinations. I tip the pup over in my hand to test his reaction. He clings tightly to my wrist. "Docile, clinging, a bit jumpy," I note next to his temporary name—Smitty—in my book.

I continue the weighing, the once-overs, the note-taking. All is well with this litter. They are rapidly gaining weight and they resemble little sumo wrestlers at this stage. They are not yet to the point of cuteness, when they begin to have more dog-like features and bolder curiosity about the world. At this age they look like the sedentary results of a cross between an obese hamster and a St. Bernard.

I let Rajah back into the brood pen and she is immediately overrun by the six hungry pups. She stands there, watching me leave, pups dangling from her underside. The look in her eyes is one of complete patience. In another week, the pups will be weaned and she will be back in the dog yard. Meanwhile, she continues to pump enough food into and out of her system to feed the litter, which together will soon weigh more than she does.

Raising puppies is one of the most delightful, tedious and exasperating aspects of keeping sled dogs. It is also one of the most essential prerequisites to fielding a team that can compete on a serious level. Visit almost any sled dog kennel, especially during the months from April through August, and you will see pups. They are the teams of the future and in addition to being athletes they may also be stepping stones to future champions by way of a planned breeding program.

After keeping sled dogs for a few seasons, mushers begin to wonder whether the phrase "breeding like rabbits," might mention the wrong kind of animal. Sled dogs are certainly fertile and willing reproducers. The fact that they travel everywhere in groups, almost always mixed groups of males and females, makes them many times more fecund than the average house pet. Also, sled dogs in working or racing teams are rarely neutered or spayed. The presumed loss of hormonal "zip" seems to convince most drivers to put up with the team's unending promiscuity. So, having sled dogs means having puppies.

Pups are born nine weeks after conception, blind but well-furred and perfectly capable of performing their required tasks—eating, sleeping and growing. During the following 15 months or so, they pass through infancy, the toddler stage, childhood, adolescence and into young adulthood. It is a remarkably rapid transition and I have never gotten over my sense of wonder at it.

Sled dog puppies have cornered the market on cuteness. They are the pups that adorn syrupy cards, calendars and clocks everywhere. They reach a magical age somewhere around seven or eight weeks, when they invariably elicit a single first response from every non-musher that sees them—a long, descending "Ohhh." At this age they are weaned from their mother, but still crave her warmth and softness. They are curious about the world but not bold enough to get into trouble. But they pass this stage, gather up their courage and begin to explore or devastate the world at large.

Only recently did I ever live in one place long enough to keep my pups in a proper pen. Year after year, I found myself in rented or seasonal residences and camps, usually with a litter or two of puppies in tow. I could always tell when their age of exploration had begun by the reports of their mischief. "Your pups were in our garden last night," or "Those damned puppies were tearing the insulation out from under the building!" or "I went under the cabin to fetch some lumber and it's just wall-to-wall puppy shit down there!"

One May morning at a tree-planting camp on Minnesota's Stony River, a couple of my friends woke after a night camped out under the stars. Somehow, their neatly folded clothing had disappeared. They quickly spotted several telling clues. A pair of jockey shorts was the object of a furious puppy tug-of-war, a brassiere was hung from an alder branch a quarter mile down the riverbank and every other piece of their clothing was strewn around the edges of the little clearing. Suddenly the pups weren't quite so cute. Still, as the Molloys scampered around collecting their wardrobes, it was impossible for all of us to keep from laughing.

The world of sled dogs is necessarily a world of puppies and it always will be. The best dogs in the world are the result of careful, long-term breeding. This is far more scientific than most people would suspect. It is not just a matter of combining "a little of this" with "a little of that." There are unplanned breedings, of course, and occasionally these produce excellent offspring. Usually, there is a plan, a "line" of dogs that is being developed and the pups that are a part of it are watched, compared, tested and chosen with care.

Pups can be the object of complex deals between dog mushers. One summer I purchased the opportunity to breed three of my females to Otter, a lead dog owned by Arleigh Jorgenson. We were going to split the litters according to first pick, second pick and so on. So, three times that summer, I brought female dogs in *estrus* over to Grand Marais aboard my tiny 1946 Cessna airplane. Each time I would buzz low over Arleigh's house and kennel to let him know I would be landing at the local airstrip in a few minutes. My dog would be left with Otter, bred and when the time was right I would bring another one over. Our joke by the end of the summer was that Otter was becoming thoroughly aroused every time he heard a small airplane overhead.

Sled dog pups, like the young of every species, live a risky, harrowing life. This is especially true in the typical backwoods setting of a dog musher's kennel. Again and again pups are lost to the various dangers and potential accidents that surround them. One pup of mine ventured down to the foam that was collecting in an eddy of the Kawishiwi River. Thinking that the white bubbles were firm snow, she blithely stepped out, was swept downstream by the current and disappeared forever under the ice that stretched out into Birch Lake. Another promising pup was investigating a musher's steaming barrel of boiled fish, tumbled into it and was horribly scalded to death.

Several times I have lost brave, naive little pups to older dogs. This seems to happen only when the pups are a certain age, about six weeks, and only with certain adults. But the dog seems to have no intention of actually eating the pup—it is simply an "unknown," and once the pup begins to squeal with terror some instinct evidently takes over and its neck is snapped. I myself killed a pup accidentally when one morning I stepped out of my cabin to find him gnawing a hole in one of my rubber boots. I plucked him off his feet and tossed him off the porch. But puppies do not have the grace and agility of kittens.

He landed sideways on his head and broke his neck. I felt terrible and foolish. Usually, the pups that meet such fates are among the best—the most courageous, inquisitive and intelligent. There are many advantages to having a large, fenced puppy pen.

I would be dishonest if I did not at some point discuss the culling of litters, the deliberate choosing of good pups—a life-and-death choice at times. Amidst all the references to breeding, improving, testing and choosing, there is an obvious question and concern: what about all the rest?

I think it would surprise many people to learn just how few pups are actually "done in"—killed—from amongst the thousands that are born in mushers' kennels each year. The act of completely discarding some litters at birth accounts for a percentage of these "culls." Unplanned, unwanted breedings do occur and always will. Even breedings that might be desirable and worthwhile can bear results at impossible times. For example, I drowned one litter at birth because they were born to my main lead dog at the start of the fall training season. Had she nursed and raised the litter, even for only four weeks, she would have been far off the pace by the time she physically recovered and rejoined the team.

There are several drugs that can be given to a female dog to abort a pregnancy following an unwanted mating. But none of them are without possible serious side effects and some are far from reliable. A hysterectomy can be performed, with obvious finality, or the litter can be taken from the mother soon after it is born. This latter approach seems to be, all in all, the most safe and healthy method. It is never pleasant, nor will it ever be. But it is necessary.

There are also those pups who are born with physical defects, some of them gross deformities, others more subtle. Many breeding efforts involve line-breeding and inbreeding. In fact, this is the way many champion dogs and champion horses have always been produced. By breeding close relatives to one another within a "line" of good dogs, the chances of combining all the desirable traits in a single pup are greatly increased. Conversely, the risk of producing dogs that show the recessive, degenerative traits is also higher in this type of breeding. These unfit dogs are not common, but they do appear. In a kennel of active, athletic dogs who travel and perform as a team, there is no humane place for a dog that is physically incapable of an athletic life.

In discussing the selection and culling of puppies, I feel somewhat defensive. This defensiveness probably stems from my own wrenching distaste for "culling" litters. I accept it as necessary and seek only to minimize the necessity for it. But if I cannot find a *good* home for a pup that cannot fit into my team, I do not keep it forever tied up in the dog yard, waiting for a chance it will never get. Also, if a litter is born and I do not have the resources or time to raise it and care for it, I will destroy it entirely. These are hard choices and not always acceptable philosophically to those people far removed from the relationship of a musher to a team, the keeping of working animals and the dedication to improving a breed in tangible, worthwhile ways.

There is an old saying in the dog world: "Those who cannot drown, should not breed." It is true. Many pups will be born and some pups will be culled. But whenever a pup is culled, there is, for me, a renewed determination to take the best possible care of the dogs I keep. I know many other mushers who share this sentiment.

The ongoing involvement of mushers and puppies is a part of dog mushing not often seen by the spectators at races or the public at large. They see trained, experienced adults performing with precision, speed and stamina. Behind each of those individual dogs, though, is an intensive period of growth, training and development. From the first time a musher sees a litter of pups, he or she is aware of them as distinct individuals and constantly on the lookout for their emerging strengths and weaknesses. The pups are the hopes of the future, the fuel for optimism about that "ultimate team" that is always coming in the years ahead.

At three days of age, the pups of a long-distance musher have their dew claws clipped off. These extra toes, partway up the front wrist, are appendages that serve no function. They may become painful and even crippling handicaps to dogs on long treks or races like the Iditarod. A protective bootie is often worn by the dogs during travel over crusty or granular snow and ice. The boot is held on at the wrist by a tight strap of Velcro or elastic. This strap can press on the nail of the dewclaw with every step the dog takes, driving it into the skin and causing a painful sore that easily becomes infected. So, when the pups are barely dry behind the ears, these two troublesome extra toes are snipped away. Already the pups have begun their preparation for the life of a long-distance dog.

Of course, sled dogs are suited for their life's work even earlier than the age of three days. Anyone who doubts the genetic basis of canine behavior has never seen a well-bred sled dog pup take to its work in harness. From the time the pups are old enough to keep pace with an old, retired lead dog, they will almost invariably work like maniacs when put in a team. Every musher has a different method of introducing pups to the sled and harness, but there are several basic requirements—patience, a slow steady pace, patience, a comfortable harness, patience, no frightening surprises and patience.

I broke all of these rules when I trained my first two pups to work in a team. I was living alone at the base camp that Lynx Track kept in a state forest in east-central Minnesota. The cabin was five or six miles from the winter roadhead and one evening I sledded out to the start of a lonesome, snow-covered logging road to put Pierre and Chiala in harness for the first time. They were already over five months old and could well have been started sooner. We had been busy and it had been put off.

Pierre and Chiala were litter mates; their mother was a Siberian husky, their father Alaskan. The five adults I had in my team that day were all veterans. My plan was to run one of the pups beside each of two older dogs and I had a hefty load in the sled to help keep the speed down. That was the theory.

Putting a harness on a frisky pup that has never worn one is often the most difficult part of the entire training process. At first, the pup has no idea what you are trying to do, shoving its head in amongst all those bands of nylon webbing that smell powerfully of the last dog who wore that harness. I had never trained a pup before, but as I wrestled with Pierre I tried to keep in mind what Duncan had told me about the process: "Just go slow, be patient and make it fun for them."

Finally, I had Pierre in his little harness and I brought him up into the team to run beside a lanky dog named Bandit. I hooked his wooden toggle to his tugline, slipped a neckline over his head and went back to where Chiala was clipped to the sled stanchion. As I picked up her harness, I caught a sidelong glimpse of Pierre just completing a one-and-a-half gainer. His toggle, neckline, Bandit's two front legs and the breast strap of Pierre's harness were all thoroughly tangled. He was whining and yipping and I was losing my patience.

Chiala was still clipped by a short lead to the stanchion of the sled. The team had come alive, urged on by Pierre's insane yapping and choking. I walked ahead, flip-flopped Pierre back into position and spoke sharply to him.

Just as I turned my attention back to Chiala, the snowhook jerked free. I made a desperate grab for the handlebar of the sled as it flew past me. I missed. Off went the team, galloping headlong down the snowy lane.

I ran behind them, steadily losing ground, until I thought I would collapse. The road was as straight as a ruler for miles and I could see the team until they topped a gentle rise and dropped over the far side. They were at least a mile ahead of me by then. I was gasping for breath, sweating in my heavy clothes, choking on frustrated words and wondering where they would finally stop.

All I remember seeing as they disappeared from view was the little furry figure of Chiala, bouncing and tumbling horribly as she was dragged by her neck behind the speeding sled. She would gain her feet for an instant and then lose her balance again, over and over. I was sure she would be killed.

I stopped for a moment after the team disappeared over the knoll. I took off my overpants, my parka, my fur hat and heavy mitts and started down the lane again at a trot.

I remembered the experience a friend of mine had just had with a lost team. A young dog of his had lost its footing when the team bolted; it had been dragged for several miles and had never regained consciousness.

In the fading twilight I crested the small hill where I had last seen the dogs. I pulled up short, amazed, wondering if I was suddenly delirious.

The team lay on the road, panting hard and looking happy, just 500 yards ahead of me. Chiala was standing up just behind the sled. Had Billy Graham walked out of the woods at that moment I would have signed on with him for life.

Somehow, as the snowhook bounced and careened along beside the sled, its sharp double claws had landed and set themselves into the snow at a rough spot in the road. The team must have slowed considerably by then. They had stopped and the snowhook looked exactly as if someone had mysteriously stepped from the underbrush and lightly kicked it into position. I glanced suspiciously around at the dark forest, shook my head and gave Pierre and Chiala a thorough, happy petting. We swung around and the new pups joined in as the team pulled for home. I can take no credit for the fact that those two both became dependable sled dogs.

Puppies keep a person honest. They mirror our moods and see through our façades. They trust us and enjoy our company only when we do the same for them. Some sled dog pups grow up in crowded, neglected pens and never achieve that trust or enjoyment of human companionship.

Somewhere between a fawning, completely "humanized" pet and a skittish wild dog lies the ideal temperament for a sled dog. This temperament combines an aloof, slightly distant nature with a strong bond to other dogs and a ready acceptance of people and their affection.

The keeping of sled dogs and the raising of their puppies involve mushers in a cycle of life and death. Within our own lifetimes, we watch many generations of dogs come into the world, grow, be trained, perform, reproduce, become old and die.

Each dog is distinctive, an individual like no other. With the dog's offspring we take part in the same cycle, again and again. Twenty years along, a musher will suddenly see a stance, a gait, or a quirk appear in some young dog; the years fall away and a nearly forgotten ancestor comes alive again in the musher's memory.

I think of these things this morning as I put away the scale and notebook and watch Rajah continue to nurse her pups. Their lives lie completely ahead of them. They are lucky, I think, to be where they are, growing toward such adventures.

DAY AFTER DAY

FOR A LONG-DISTANCE DOGTEAM, TRAINING IS THE name of the game. A team can be composed of the best individual dogs in the world, fed the finest diet, bank-rolled by the wealthiest sponsors and be driven by a canny, experienced musher, but without training they will never run like champions. Conversely, a ragtag group of mongrels and culls, skimping along on meager, mismatched rations, funded by an overdue bank note and driven by a stubborn, determined novice can, with proper training, put in a performance that will surprise the mushing world. It is unlikely that this latter team could actually win any major race these days, but such teams can and do make respectable showings. This is one of the beauties of sled dog sport—if a person is willing to work hard and pay the required dues of miles, months and hard knocks, he or she can advance rapidly into professional-caliber competition.

Training, as it applies to dog mushing, takes place within several different meanings of the word. Mention dog training to the owner of the neighborhood poodle and it connotes the mastery of obedience, good house manners, perhaps fetching slippers or the newspaper. To a marathon runner, training means mileage, speed work, stretching and a gradual building up of endurance. For a ball player, there is the added element of teamwork, the practicing of plays, the perfection of timing. For the musher preparing a dogteam for a long-distance event, training combines elements of all of these—from dog obedience to physical endurance to teamwork.

About the time that several leaves on the smallest birches begin to show a tinge of yellow, late August in most sled dog climates, the thoughts of mushers turn to the start of training. Nowadays, most teams are kept in reasonable physical fitness even over the height of summer, with mechanical "walkers," free running, or short sled pulls on bare ground. But actual training, the steady buildup to peak performance, begins as summer ends. The first snow of winter is many weeks or even several months away when a musher and a team have to "get serious."

A hilarious and horrifying book could be written from the stories mushers tell of early season training. A photo album would overflow with snapshots of the training carts that have been designed, demolished and scrapped over the years. My team has pulled me in September and October on rigs ranging from Lynx Track's flimsy little "suicide buggy" to a Volkswagen chassis complete with bucket seats, tape deck and a marginally functional steering wheel. In between were several bastardized combinations involving automobile axles, motorcycle handlebars and all-terrain vehicles.

I have cursed at, repaired and finally sold or junked them all. At the large end of the scale was my entire pickup truck itself, idling along in second gear with ten or 20 dogs in harness out in front. For sheer simplicity, there was the unforgettable ride I took one October evening, clinging desperately to a rope behind 17 galloping dogs. I was dragged about a half mile before Kristen caught up to me with the truck. This, of course, saved wear and tear on cart tires, but my shredded coveralls did not hold up very well.

Perhaps cart training, so necessary to physically prepare a team for a winter of races, serves an even more important function. As a musher and a team of dogs face the mud, sand, squeaking axles and flat tires of the season's beginning, they are mentally toughened for the winter runs and races ahead. It is a time for testing dogs and training methods, for clearing out the mental cobwebs. Over the summer, I eagerly anticipate the start of training, the means and rewards of which are idealized in my imagination. A few bouts of cart training never fail to put things back into proper perspective. I remember the wry advice of a fellow musher: "When the going gets tough . . . the smart go shopping."

I never had much need to do any serious cart training, or "dirt training" as it is sometimes called, until I began to compete in long-distance races. In the years when my dogs and I would spend winters guiding and teaching in Minnesota's north woods, the physical condition of our human clients usually limited our travels long before the dogs were played out. Our daily mileage on courses was minimal; sometimes not even ten miles were covered in a full day of travel. The dogs gradually became conditioned over the course of the season and by spring they were tough enough for any long trek we might decide to make.

But with my attempts to compete seriously in the Beargrease race and the Iditarod, my approach to early season training had to change. The Beargrease is run in mid-January and sometimes even by then the snow cover is barely sufficient for sledding in northern Minnesota. Training for a race hundreds of miles long must begin at least three, and preferably four to six, months before the start. So after I had selected, purchased and leased my team for that first season of racing, I had to locate a workable training rig.

I found a training cart that suited my needs in the barn of a retired dog musher in central Minnesota. It was a solid-looking combination—the rear axle of a Rambler joined to the front fork of a Harley Davidson. It came "loaded," of course—complete with a locking hand brake, in a lusterless red paint and with tires that held air for upwards of seven hours between refills. I moved my dogs and gear to a backwoods tent camp where my friend Bert Hyde and I were working on his log house. Early in the morning, all through September and one of the wettest Octobers on record, I would stumble out into the muddy clearing and hook up two successive teams for runs down six or eight miles of the rutted, puddle-filled road. During the day Bert and I would work on his cabin. In the evenings we would puzzle over how to repair the latest damage to the cart.

Ice was a big problem. The temperature was well below freezing on some mornings, but the road's deep mud holes would not freeze solidly. As we splashed through puddle after icy puddle, the spray would freeze on the cart's brake mechanism. Finally I perfected the technique of pointing a stream of processed coffee, warm from my bladder, precisely onto the frozen cable linkage of the brake—all while careening down the lane at 12 miles an hour. Necessity, invention and all that . . . I'm glad no one ever saw me in the midst of *that* process!

One night in late October the weather turned so cold that the entire running gear of the cart was frozen solid. We built a huge bonfire and dragged the cart up next to it to thaw before the morning training runs. I muttered something about how I had thought that when I became a dog musher I had moved a step away from axles, brake fluid and flat tires. Bert, who does not think very highly of sled dog competitions, put it all in perspective: "You aren't dog mushing anymore, man. You're playing pro baseball."

He was right. By requiring that we begin training months before the season of snow and sleds arrives, the sport of dog mushing enters a new dimension. Perhaps if we all moved up to a glacier for the summer. . .

Dogs begin the training season in a burst of frantic enthusiasm. Every time the cart or chassis or sled is pulled into position the dog yard erupts with the mad clamor of barks, howls, screams and whines. As each dog is led into position and harnessed in the team, the decibel level increases. Even the start of a January race, with eighteen dogs in a team, does not compare to the absolute bedlam of a five-dog team ready to tear out of the yard in early September. Gradually, though, the dogs accustom themselves to the training regimen and the start of each run becomes a bit more manageable.

Somewhere along the way toward 1,000 miles of training, most teams go into a predictable slump. They walk out to their places in harness and sit quietly or even lie down until it is time to go. They leave the dog yard at a half-interested trot instead of their usual gallop. For the musher who has never seen this slump and accompanied a team through it, it is a nerve-wracking time. One wonders if the dogs will ever recover their zest, their fire.

I had heard of this predictable slump before I first encountered it with my own team. "Take them through it," I'd been advised. "They have to learn that they have to go even when they don't feel like it."

As training techniques continue to evolve, I don't hear so much of this advice, this insistence on pushing the dogs right through the worst of their "sour" periods. Probably, given the independent nature of dog mushers, no consensus will ever emerge as to the training of a team. It seems more important to have a personal plan and to stick to it consistently than to have adopted, verbatim, some standard training formula.

The low point of the dog's enthusiasm seems to hit my team somewhere around the 600-mile mark. As each dog's training mileage approaches that figure, usually in early December, their eagerness declines. The slump itself can be precipitated then by a single run that is too long, by a spell of extremely cold or warm weather, or by snow conditions that make the trail surface irritating to the dogs' feet.

An experienced Alaskan musher once remarked to me on how similar the process of training sled dogs is to the training of young human athletes. Catie Maloney had been a competitive swimmer in high school. One day, while mushing a team of yearlings down the trail, she realized that she was doing exactly the sorts of things that her swimming coach had done—pushing, backing off, encouraging, inspiring, cajoling, driving hard, resting. "I finally realized what that coach had been doing to us!" she laughed.

But even personal, full-time Olympic coaches do not have any closer involvement with their athletes than good mushers have with their dogs. Since dogs are dogs and cannot have the training process "explained" to them through logic or reason, we must simply make every aspect of the dog's training experience as correct as we can.

Dogs live in the present tense. Preparation for a race three months ahead is a concept far beyond the scope of their mental capacities. What they know—all they know—is what is happening now and how it correlates with their established patterns of habit, instinct and association. We decide nearly everything for them as we go through the training process: where to run, when to run, when to rest, what to feed, which dogs run best in which positions and on and on. It is a complicated, fascinating process that goes far beyond the simple discipline of hooking up a team, day after day.

Dogs are individuals and they take to training in ways that reflect their own temperament, physical condition and age. Dogs that have been trained again and again, old veterans of many races, do not need nearly as many training miles as do younger, less experienced dogs. In fact, any dog can be "overtrained," just as a human

athlete can. If a musher pushes too hard, out of enthusiasm and stubborn adherence to a schedule, the result
can be a team that is actually tired before it even starts
a race. In training dogteams, as in so many endeavors,
quality counts for more than quantity.

As for mushers and their own physical training,
there is no typical pattern. Some drivers make an effort
to maintain and to improve their fitness in preparation
for racing. Others, sometimes equally successful, do not.
The life of keeping and training a long-distance dogteam
is physically demanding in and of itself. Some mushers
add their own running, stretching and calisthenics to the
team's overall training regimen and doubtless such efforts
pay off on the trail. But at its heart the competition is
between dogs. The "toughness" demanded of mushers
is at least as much mental as it is physical. In this sport,
we humans are the coaches, the managers and the strat-
egists more than the actual players.

My first season of training for races was a year when
the snow did not come to Minnesota until nearly New
Year's Day. That year cart training accounted for over
600 miles of each dog's preseason running. Considering
that I always ran my 16 dogs in at least two smaller teams,
the cart and I put on at least 1,200 "dirt miles" that
season. Sometime around Christmas, thoroughly sick of
mud and puddles and tires, I vowed that in years to come
I would go north to find snow earlier in the fall. For two
years after that, Mike Dietzman, the dogs and I all headed
for northern Manitoba, to a cabin on the Churchill River
near Leaf Rapids, to get a head start on winter. Both
years, of course, Minnesota received a heavy snowfall
within days after our departure.

Once we were settled into our routine on the
Churchill, though, I realized that the real advantage of
moving away from home in search of good training conditions was not the chance of earlier cold and snow. The
advantage was the move itself. We left behind not only
warm weather and muddy roads, but jobs, phones and

outside commitments. We were there for one purpose—to train sled dogs.

Even at 57 degrees north latitude in the mid-continental cold belt, we were rushing the season a bit by trying to train with sleds in early November. Once we broke through the treacherous shore-fast ice of the Churchill River and gave ourselves and five dogs a frigid, frightening swim. Often in our daily jaunts across the huge expanses of Granville Lake, we had the eerie experience of sledding over a thin sheet of perfectly clear black ice, only three inches thick but already tremendously strong. The increasing darkness, the deepening cold, the lack of proper shelter for the dogs—those Novembers were a hardening-up period for all of us in ways that went beyond the mileage figures recorded in the team's logbook.

Consider a day of training at our camp on the Churchill in November 1985.

In the dark, the alarm clock rings. I smash down its lever and force myself partly out from under the warm covers—a hedge against falling back to sleep. As I cool off, I gradually wake up. I find the pump handle of the Coleman lamp, give it a few quick strokes, fumble for a lighter and turn on the gas. The lantern hisses and a weak yellow light throws flickering shadows around the small room. I swing upright, grab for my trousers and sweater and quickly pull them on. Dietz groans from the loft above, hearing the lantern and my movements. When the lamp begins to burn brightly I hoist it up to its hanger near the ceiling. I shine a flashlight out the window at the thermometer dial. "Minus 32 degrees Fahrenheit . . . positively tropical out there," I call up to Dietz.

"Swimsuit weather," he mumbles.

I stuff the stove full of paper and kindling and with its drafts wide open it soon begins to roar. "Only 25 above in here," I tell him. "Maybe we should be down sleeping with the dogs."

"Yeah. Right."

Soon a big pot of coffee is perked and I, an incurable addict, stare out the window at pitch blackness, listening to the CBC radio report of the day's news. When the weather forecast begins we both lean forward slightly. "For Lynn Lake, Leaf Rapids, South Indian Lake today, brisk northwesterly winds giving windchills over 2,000 watts per square meter, partly cloudy with a few sunny breaks and a chance of flurries."

"That," Mike chuckles, "tells me precisely nothing." We laugh and pour more coffee. The announcer's pronunciation of windchill sounds like windshield and we have started a long-standing joke about the "windshield factor," involving square meters of plexiglass, watts and brisk winds.

"That dog water on?"

"You bet."

"O.K., I'm going to water those poor potlickers."

He climbs into a pair of heavy coveralls, a down coat, a fur hat and huge gauntlet mitts, straps a headlamp to his forehead and picks up the kettle of rich-smelling liver and chicken broth. He is out the door in a fog of frost and it slams behind him.

Twenty minutes later he is back, puffing from his climb up the esker, giving me the report on everyone as I stir a pot of oatmeal. "Tom's shaking like a leaf down there, but he always does that. Arnold's still limping."

"Hmmm. Well, I guess old Arnie Schwarzenegger's got another day off."

By the time we finish breakfast, daylight has begun to show on the southeast horizon. It is 8:15. We begin the ritual of preparing for the day's 35-mile run. Both of us bundle heavily in warm clothing, a lunch is packed, three thermoses of tea and chocolate are filled and enough serviceable dog booties are salvaged out of the long strings of them hanging from the rafters. I have jotted the two teams, dog by dog, on two slips of paper and I give one to Dietz. He studies it as if he's just been dealt a poker hand. Then he nods. Evidently he approves of his roster. On some days we spar a bit over who will run which dogs, who will leave first and so on.

We each pull the harnesses for our teams from the bundle of them that hangs that near the stove and that adds considerably to the fragrance inside the cabin. Each dog has its own harness, fit according to length, girth and overall build. The entire assortment is a motley variety of styles, colors and ages. In a small warm room, they create quite a bouquet.

Out the door and down to the dogs. They are tethered along a narrow band of alders on the shore of a small frozen backwater of the Churchill. It is a dark, cold spot for them at this time of the year, but there is no alternative. They bark as we approach down the hill. A few stand and shake themselves.

Within 20 minutes, each of 64 paws has been fitted with a cloth bootie. The surface conditions of the lake ice are terrible in this deep cold. The windblown snow and jagged ice have begun to take a toll on the team's footpads. So each morning, everyone gets four booties. Like the harnesses, these come in a wide assortment of colors, materials and styles. The dogs are by now accustomed to wearing their booties and they are well-behaved as we fit each of them with a set.

"You going out first?"

"No, why don't you let Morrie take them out today. I know he'll go." After a long run yesterday, under miserable conditions, I am not confident that my leader, Tex, will set an inspiring pace out of the dog yard. He has been known to balk on days like this and there is no more demoralizing way to start a run than with a hesitant leader.

We move quickly, as the sun sends cold angled light across the spruce tops. Soon our two eight-dog teams are in place. Arnold, Henry and Eddie all watch from their spots along the tie-out cable. Henry has a slight cough, Eddie has been favoring a shoulder and Arnold is still getting over an injured toe. They will keep a cold vigil here while their teammates are out running.

After the bustle of hitching up the teams, we both pause to put on our final layers of clothing—wind parkas, fur hats and heavy mittens on "idiot strings." We cinch our cuffs, snug up our drawstrings and fit soft woolen faceguards over our noses and cheeks. The first blast of cold air can bite deeply into the tip of an exposed nose as the dogs speed out of the yard. And once we hit the river, there will be those "brisk" northwesterlies.

Mike turns toward me, looking like an astronaut trussed up for a moon walk and I give him a wave that says "go ahead." He pulls his snub line loop from around a post of the canoe rack and old Morris leads the team out. I watch them go, carefully studying each dog. They seem all right—happy and eager. My own team, as expected, is suddenly on fire with the urge to chase their buddies down the lake. When Mike has rounded a slight bend in the shoreline a half mile down, I give Tex the word and we are off.

Morris keeps his team in the lead, as we had hoped he would. I stop several times in the first few miles, to switch some dogs to different positions and to replace one of D. J.'s booties. We are passing through a maze of narrow, unplowed roads, then a closed summer campground, before I pull within sight of Mike's team again. He is stopped and I stop my team far behind him. I can tell he is in the midst of bawling out a little female, Christie, who is running in wheel. He has her head lifted and is shouting into her face like a third baseman telling the umpire what he thought of *that* call. With a little swat to her nose, he steps to one side and the team charges ahead. He swings onto the sled as it shoots past him.

At the start of the portage around an open set of rapids, we each anchor our snowhooks among some scattered boulders. We walk ahead and release the dogs' tuglines from the toggles at the back of their harnesses. Only the leaders are left to pull properly; everyone else is running only on their necklines. With the teams' power and speed thus drastically reduced, we ease over the rocky, twisted trail that is still in desperate need of more snow. At its far end is a dramatic 20-foot drop onto the ice of Granville Lake—definitely not a trail to negotiate at top speed.

Once out on Granville, with the teams restored to full power, we catch the unchecked force of the wind. The dogs are angling across it, so it will be an equal factor on our return trip. Miniature funnel clouds of spindrift scurry across the trail. The teams move steadily, trotting about nine miles an hour and Mike and I each crouch low on the runners, our faces turned from the blast. It won't be a day for much finesse in training.

About 90 minutes out of camp, I catch up to Mike. Coming past him, I call sharply to my leader, "All right, Tex. On by, on by! Get up there!" I underscore the words with a vigorous rattling of my jingler. This is a noisemaker, a dozen bottle caps strung on a metal ring. It is my accelerator, about midway in effectiveness between verbal commands and the sharp crack of a signal whip.

Tex takes his team smoothly past and does not let the pace fall off after the incentive of the chase has disappeared. He is doing well.

"Good boy, atta boy," I shout.

Two hours out, as we thread our way along a narrows at the base of tall granite cliffs, I stop my team. Mike pulls in just behind me and we both pound our snowhooks into the clear black ice.

"How they doing?"

"Pretty good—a lot better than I thought. When we came through the campground they were really motorin'. I swear Tom must have been *trotting* 17 miles an hour!"

The teams get a snack here and we take a 20-minute rest. The "liver cookies," actually frozen dollops of chicken hearts and livers, are snapped out of the air by every dog. We disconnect their toggles from the tuglines again so that they can curl up completely for their short naps. Then we hunker down on the lee side of Mike's sled for our own lunch and several cups of hot chocolate and tea.

"You staying warm enough?"

"Oh, yeah. I pulled out all the stops today."

"Me too."

We don't say much during our breaks. Each of us is thinking, munching a handful of nuts, sipping from our cup. Twenty minutes pass quickly and soon we are tossing things back into our sleds, hooking up toggles and preparing to take off again.

The wind has increased a little and veered north. The sky is completely overcast now and though it is midday the sunlight is dim and faltering. It is nearly the first of December. In another week we will be far south, in Minnesota. In six weeks, the Beargrease race will be over and with luck we'll be headed for Alaska. My thoughts wander widely as we make our way home.

This may be our last long run on Granville Lake. The dogs will get a day off tomorrow and then two days of shorter, more varied runs along the highway near town. I turn to look back at Mike. He too is looking over his shoulder, back toward the distant shapes of two low, dark islands we call "The Battleships."

By the looks of this team, I have not made the mistake that I have made in other seasons, pushing too hard, demanding too much. They are running steadily, undaunted by the strong crosswind, confident and trustful that we are bound home by the most direct route. Two hours and ten minutes after leaving our lunch break we each set our snowhooks around the posts alongside the dog yard.

"I got 2:10 coming in," Mike says, "Two-even going out."

"That's what I got, too. I couldn't quite get them rolling as we came in through the campground there."

"Yeah, me neither."

Now I hurry up the hill to our cabin and return with a five-gallon bucket of warm broth, similar to what the dogs were given at daybreak. While they are still in harness, they each get a bowl and lap eagerly at it, two-by-two down the line of each team.

We stand and watch them drink. These few moments are a choice part of each training day. The run is over, the dogs are slurping their broth, the sun is low in the southwest.

When they have finished, we stack up the battered metal bowls. We both remove the booties from our dogs, piling the torn ones separately from those that are still usable. Each dog is hustled back to its place, patted and spoken to. The sleds are tugged into position, heading out. We gather up harnesses, lunch pack and booties. We climb back up the trail to the cabin.

Nothing dramatic has gone on today—no high-speed chase or near-disaster. It has been just another cold, windy training run. The dogs have done well. Some of them performed superbly, others less so.

Back inside, we stoke the fire and peel off our layers of insulation. I make another trip down to the river to chop open our ice hole and haul up two pails of water. Mike starts cooking dinner. I mix the tub of dog food, going heavy on the chicken fat as the cold weather continues.

The long hours of darkness begin. By quarter to four the lamp is hissing away again. At six, the dogs are fed and we eat our own supper as we listen to the chatter of "As It Happens" on the radio. After dinner, Dietz is engrossed in beading the mukluks he is making for his girlfriend. I am reading the Beargrease Race statistics sheets of the past two years, writing down the outline of some teams' runs, rests and speeds from checkpoint to checkpoint.

"Trying to figure out a way to beat teams that are twice as fast as yours?" Mike asks.

"That's about it."

Long silence. The sound of beads being sorted. Wind in jack pines. The scratch of pencil on paper.

"Well, fun-hogs, it's 8:30. Way past my bedtime. I'll see you in the a.m.," Mike says.

"Yeah, okay. Day off tomorrow. I'm going to walk into town. I've got 19 sled dogs down there in the yard and I'm going to walk to town. Can you believe it?" I ask.

"Well, if they're getting a day off, we may as well take one too. I'll walk with you. Anything that doesn't involve so much as *looking* at a dog!"

"Okay. Good night."

"G'night."

I stay up a while longer, enjoying the solitude and staring at the blackness outside the window, letting my mind drift. I am full of a pleasant, warm fatigue. Another day of training is over.

'TIL THEY DROP

J OHN BEARGREASE MUST BE ROLLING IN HIS GRAVE. I TRY to conjure up an image of the old Ojibway dog driver wandering through the crowd here at the start of the race that bears his name ... his tattered parka, greasy moosehide mitts, weather-beaten face and a look of absolute astonishment in his dark eyes. But the image won't stay. It is an exercise in futility to try to envision his reaction to the scene tonight.

Ordean School, in the heart of Duluth, Minnesota, is a noisy place this January evening, January 7, 1987. There is loud rock music in the air, or at least there had been up to the time when teams began making their way to the starting chute. Right now, there is only a clamorous mingling of sounds, as if someone had jumbled together the sound tracks from "Sergeant Preston," "Monday Night Football" and the Kentucky Derby. It could be only one thing—the start of a long-distance sled dog race. Thirty-two dogteams will be leaving here tonight, two-by-two.

The John Beargrease Sled Dog Marathon is an annual race along the north shore of Lake Superior in northern Minnesota. Its total mileage varies from year to year but is always more than 350 miles. Actually, to say that the race follows the lake's north shore can be misleading. No running is done on the lake ice itself. Instead the trail hugs the crest of the coastal hills, rugged Precambrian roots of an ancient mountain range, thickly wooded with pine, birch and maple. The racecourse descends, again and again, into various settlements, crossroads and communities along the shore. It has a well-deserved reputation among mushers as a difficult, demanding trail, yet it is also one of the most "civilized" of the major long-distance events, with road access to every checkpoint and crowds of spectators around bonfires, watching along the way.

Here we go again. Time to put up or shut up. Lean and mean. My mind fills with such banal clichés as the minutes pass. Two teams are already out on the trail. We have drawn starting position #11 for the run out of Duluth; there are still 13 minutes to go before we leave the chute. I feel the tight knot in my gut that will only gradually dissolve over the next 60 to 70 hours, worn away by fatigue and the passage of many miles.

Merv Hilpipre chatters along in his auctioneer's voice, with the color commentary: "And now into the starting area is Joe Redington, Senior, from Wasilla, Alaska, the Father of the Iditarod Trail Race. Joe is running two very experienced lead dogs out of here tonight and. . . ." I lose the rest of the sentence as another screaming, leaping string of dogs is led past me toward the chute.

Two assistant judges approach, flustered and obviously behind their schedule. They quickly check the gear in my sled: axe, snowshoes, dog booties, trail rations, sleeping bag, promotional mailbag, first aid kit. Their mood is perfunctory. "Good luck, Dave." My name and number are crossed off their list.

Around the truck, the three people who will be my handlers for the race are busy planning and organizing their tasks and equipment. Now, in these moments before the start, I feel oddly separated from them. These are my trusted friends, people I love—Kristen, Dietz and my sister Nanci. We will be a close-knit team for the next three days or more, yet we face different aspects of the same goal: to get this team of dogs up the north shore trail and back to Duluth in the fastest possible time and in the best possible condition. There is a subtle distance between us as the race begins, a professional detachment. I have become the "driver" and they the "handlers." They work as a team in the checkpoints while I, with the dogs, move toward them along the trail.

I crave that coming solitude. I am desperately eager to be out in the dark, away from these lights, this noise and this crowd, eager to watch my team move swiftly down the starlit trail. To let the race unfold.

Suddenly I catch sight of a smiling and long-familiar face in the glow spilling over from the floodlights. She makes her way toward me through the crowd. I suddenly feel sheepish. My fancy red nylon coverall is festooned with sponsor's logos and topped by a clean numbered bib. My headlamp and battery pack, the sleek blue sled bag and delicate racing sled—all these *things* seem so far removed from the hard-bitten world of the winter trail. Margie knows me from years ago, years when those first seven dogs and I shared a small camp in the north woods, eating oatmeal and whitefish, rolling Drum tobacco, living close to the bone and proudly detached from the atmosphere that surrounds us tonight. Perhaps she has just now realized what the outer appearances of this racing scene involve. I wonder and worry, what this trusted friend thinks of all this glitter.

"Good luck," she says with a hug. "You look pretty flashy."

From her manner, I get the impression that she understands, that it doesn't matter, that it's still just a musher and a dogteam and the trail, as always. I quote my friend Bob Saviganc, a man we both know well, who always claims, "If you're gonna act like one, you may as well look like one." We laugh.

I have a confession to make. I find it difficult to trust all this hype, this noise and flash and color. It is too *American,* too directly tied to the exact opposites of all the things I like about mushing dogs. It seems superficial. I fear that the essence of the endeavor will flounder out of sight in this carnival atmosphere. But now the race is on. In a moment, this scene will be peripheral.

Ten minutes. Time to move. The dogs are already in harness, standing around the truck with their booties on. Official paint marks on their shoulders give them the unmistakable look of racers. They know what is happening. Despite my constant admonitions against giving the dogs more human characteristics than they possess, I know that at moments like these they have a sense of the tension, the anticipation, that flows from all of us crazy humans.

"This ain't gonna be just another training run, boys," I can almost hear my crusty old leader, Beaver, whispering to his younger partners around the rear bumper. "This is the real McCoy tonight, balls to the wall. . . ."

His imagined words of wisdom are cut short as the four of us swarm around the truck, unclipping dogs and leading them forward by the collar to their positions in the team. Tonight, only nine dogs will leave Duluth. The trail conditions have been deemed unsafe for full-strength racing teams, because of the scant snow cover and the many road crossings and intersections in the first 40 miles. At Highway Two, north of Two Harbors, we will each take a mandatory rest stop and from there we can proceed with our full teams of up to 20 dogs.

Five minutes. I buckle the cover on the sled bag, clicking my headlamp on and off for the hundredth time to make sure that it works. Kristen and I stand at the sled and a crew of helpers station themselves alongside each dog in the team. "Well, we'll see you in a few hours. We won't be stopping at the Idle Hour."

"Have a good run," she says with a smile and a peck on the cheek. "Smoke 'em."

An official steps toward us from the direction of the starting chute. "Ready, Dave? Bring them up." I stand with both feet on the brake and tug the snowhook loose from the bumper of the truck. We clumsily ease forward, the helpers each struggling to hold back a jumping, excited dog. At this stage I feel like a space capsule atop a launch pad, with all these helpers, snow fences and crowds being the booster stages that will soon fall away and let us fly out into the night.

Our halting procession slows to a stop at the starting line itself. Four or five burly fellows take hold of the stanchions of the little basket sled. The snowhook is set into an old truck tire, which in turn is cabled in place. The helpers continue to stand by the dogs.

"One minute," blares the loudspeaker.

I walk ahead along the team, talking steadily to the dogs and clapping my hands softly.

This serves absolutely no purpose. The dogs are eager to go; they need no encouragement from me. More important is the visual check I make of everyone's tugline, harness and neckline and the quick glance ahead down the chute.

Parallel to us in the opposite starting chute is Dave Shyne from Duluth and his dogteam. I wave hello to him. We have already agreed that I will try to clear the start area with my team first. This dual start is mostly a matter of expediency; it provides a colorful flavor of competition at the start, but it doesn't matter one iota who gets to the end of the 100-foot starting lane first, with hundreds of miles of trail ahead.

Finally, I am back at the sled and the countdown from 10 is in progress.

Now I turn deaf to the din around me.

All I hear are the numbers of the timer. The helpers alongside the dogs step back to each side.

The team jumps and barks and the sled shakes with the strain. I loop my mittened hand through a rope on the handlebar—a sure bet to dislocate my shoulder if I do fall off.

The men holding the sled say something cheerful to me; I nod. "Three, two. . ."

"Ready, Morris! Beaver!"

"Go!"

"All right! All right!"

Finally, we're off. The team gallops out from beneath the lights and the sled swings into a wide left turn onto a snow-covered street. About a quarter mile down, we turn right and climb a series of hills through what looks like a park or golf course. It feels wonderful to be underway. I say nothing to the dogs.

Virtually this whole first night of the race I will be silent except to direct them gee or haw or to start and stop. Encouraging them to run faster now is self-defeating. If anything, I would say, "Back off there, my friends, it's a long haul." That command, however, is not in their repertoire, so I am quiet.

We climb the long hills out of Duluth, gradually putting the lights of the city and the harbor far below and behind us. The trail is indeed tricky in places. I feel glad to be running a manageable team of nine dogs.

We are racing now and I feel it. Within my usual thoughts when running a dogteam at night there is the added flare of the aggression of competition. Seconds count, as I learned one year in a race in eastern Ontario, finishing three seconds behind Pete Sapin's second-place team and seven minutes behind the winner, Arleigh Jorgenson, after 18 hours on the trail. That was an important lesson for me. Now I strive never to forget that a race is just that—*a race.*

Ten miles out we pass through the Idle Hour checkpoint in a tight cluster of other teams, none of which pause there. From there the race begins to stretch out along the North Shore Trail, a wide boulevard through the woods, designed and maintained for snowmobile riders. The night is pleasantly cool and the next 38 miles to Highway Two pass quickly, with the front cluster of teams beginning to overtake and be passed by each other as the dogs settle into their respective cruising speeds.

I have the easy job now. I imagine my helpers up ahead at the checkpoint, busily preparing for our arrival. There we will hitch up the remainder of the team, nine more dogs, tend to the ones that will already have come 50 miles and catch our breath a bit after the intense concentration of the start. While my crew is driving, parking, starting stoves and laying out ganglines, I stand on the runners and listen to the steady panting of my dogs in the darkness.

At 11:28 p.m., about four hours out of the Idle Hour, we sign into the Highway Two checkpoint. Because of the addition of dogs to the teams, we will all stay here for a minimum of one hour. To this will be added any time differentials needed to make up for our staggered starts, so from here to the finish line, whoever is first on the trail is leading the race.

I am nervous about this impending change from nine to 18 dogs. I have never added nine fresh dogs to a team that had already come 50 miles.

We decide to cluster the new dogs near the rear of the team, with the hope that the front pairs will set a reasonable pace. Still, as we pull away from the checkpoint and make a harrowing crossing of a narrow wooden bridge, I feel like I am driving a very disjointed dogteam, with a constant tendency to tumble up and over itself.

I know for certain that I do not have the fastest team of dogs in this race. Joe Garnie is here and Myron Angstman and Joe Redington, all from Alaska. There are Robin Jacobson, Jamie Nelson, Linwood Fiedler and Tim White to contend with, as well as threatening unknown teams. My strategy is to move out to the head of the pack early, in hopes of running with the top teams and letting the race evolve from there. The danger in such a plan is to push too hard in the early portion of the race. There is precious little time for rest and recovery later on. It is a balancing act and it never becomes easy or predictable.

A pair of chance meetings along the trail out of Highway Two do not help me to remain objective about my team's position and capabilities. I come to a fork in the trail and in the darkness I am not certain which of the two routes has been marked for the race. I kick in my snowhook and another one alongside it and walk cautiously forward to see if tracks on the trail might give me a clue. As I scan the two trails with my headlamp beam, the eerie spectacle of a long file of glowing dog eyes pulls into sight behind me. It is Myron Angstman's team.

"Got a problem?"

"Well, I'm just not sure which of these trails we take."

"Oh. Well, I can't hold mine. I think it's this other one. Haw there, haw!" And he's gone.

That, I reflect, is the sort of decision-making that wins and loses races.

I follow the other route, convinced that I remember using it in years past. Less than a half mile farther on, the two trails merge again into a single well-marked path. The kick I give myself gives the team an extra boost.

The trail enters a stretch of rolling hills and crosses several watersheds. Along a thickly wooded section I abruptly come upon another team and again it is Angstman. "I need help here. Can you give me a hand?" I set my snowhook around a tree and trot forward.

"I got a dog choking here, tangled up. Can you put some slack in the gangline from the front?" In a moment the dog is free, the tangle is unraveled and Angstman is ready to go.

"You need a hand here, Dave?"

I tell him I can make it across—the trail is flooded with water and his team had balked as they waded through it. "Thanks a lot." He is away into the darkness.

It is 3 a.m. I have a small mix-up getting my team across the water, but soon we are underway.

My thoughts are all with Angstman. He has one of the best middle- to long-distance teams in the world. We seem to be running with him. I am encouraged, dangerously so.

At 5:16 a.m. we arrive at the Finland checkpoint, 87 miles into the race. My crew is there, ready and organized and cheerful. They are taking turns sleeping at the checkpoints—I see only Nanci and Kristen. I drop Tom here, a good fast male who had been injured just ten days before the race in a scrap with Morris. He is limping slightly and has diarrhea. He could conceivably recover on the run, but I am not hopeful, so his race is over.

Joe Garnie, surely one of the major contenders in this race, strolls by my resting team. He is cheerful and casual, as always. "Whose team is this?" he asks my sister. She points to me and Joe walks over. "Shit, Dave, they're not tired, huh?"

"Nope. Not really." I doubt that Joe is trying to play mental games with me. But if he is, he is succeeding. I am encouraged again. According to plan, we pull out of Finland after a 30-minute rest, the first team on the trail.

Linwood Fiedler from Montana pulls out with me and we travel together for a few miles. He stops to change a dog's position or fix a tangled line and we ease ahead of him. From what I can see, his team and mine are fairly evenly matched at this stage of the game.

The stretch of trail between Finland and the Sawbill Road checkpoint is notorious for its seemingly endless steep hills. Again and again, the team plummets into the very bottom of a ravine, only to slowly, grudgingly climb out again. It can be an especially grueling section if traversed in the warmth of a sunny afternoon, after an all-night run from Duluth. I am determined, this year, to put it behind us in the cooler hours of morning.

On the Beargrease, as on almost every long sled dog race, there are mandatory rest stops. As on the Iditarod Trail, the longest Beargrease rest is taken at a checkpoint chosen by the musher. Every race gradually develops a classic strategy, from which teams make creative and sometimes radical departures. But the Beargrease is still a young race. Its total length and the rules regarding rests have changed greatly from year to year.

Thus, no classic strategy has yet emerged. The choice of where to take the long rest stop is one of the major decisions a team must make. Behind us on this Thursday morning, Joe Garnie is already taking his eight hours in Finland. I plan to rest my team at Sawbill and take off from there in the twilight of early evening.

It is no secret among mushers that sled dogs on long races run faster at night. This is a fact that goes beyond optical illusion. It is cooler at night and there are less distractions for the dogs on a dark trail. Perhaps it is a throwback to night hunting by the dog's wolf ancestors. Whatever the reason, daylight and darkness are factors that strongly influence the running and resting strategies of most racers.

About 15 miles from the Sawbill checkpoint, I am passed in rapid succession by Robin Jacobson and Myron Angstman. Their teams look strong and steady as they go by.

Robin is concerned by some blood he has seen on the trail. Makepeace, one of my little females, has been nipped in the nostril by her cantankerous running mate, Banjo, and she has inhaled a little of the blood. She is sneezing and coughing; I will have to drop her at Sawbill.

At 9:55 on Thursday morning, I sign into Sawbill checkpoint. I am not obliged by the rules to declare that this will be our eight-hour layover spot, though I know it will be. My handlers begin dodging a few curious in-

quiries from the other teams' crews and interested onlookers. Eventually, as mid-afternoon passes, it is clear to
everyone that we intend to remain here for a full eight
hours. Myron is taking his long rest here, as is Joe Redington. Fiedler, Jacobson and Nelson have all charged
ahead toward Grand Marais.

The team is tired. We wrap them all in bright red
warm-up jackets and bed them down on piles of dry straw
in the quiet spruce woods. I sleep for a few hours and
wake feeling stiff, groggy and generally worse than I did
before the nap. As I loiter around the truck in the half-
daze of awakening, a woman wearing a race bib marked
"Veterinarian" approaches and greets me.

"Uh, Dave, we need to get a blood test from you."

My sister chimes in. "From *him?* He's already half
anemic. Another teaspoon gone and we'll never get him
out of here!"

The vet laughs and continues, "If we can just choose
a dog here, I'll get what we need and get out of your
hair."

"Sure, no problem. Pick any one."

We walk together over to my resting team and the
vet decides that D.J. will be the guinea pig today. He is
poked in the foreleg and a small vial fills rapidly with
dark venous blood. D.J. watches the whole process sleepily and dozes off again.

Testing for prohibited drugs is now standard pro-
cedure in major dog races. It is a painless, efficient way
to ensure "clean racing" by all teams. Of equal importance, it is a valuable response to the cluck-cluck criticism
of the sport's detractors, who would gladly have the
world believe that all teams are "doped." As a racer, I
am always glad for the testing effort and happy to have
my dogs checked.

At 5:55 in the evening, with 16 dogs in the team,
I sign out of Sawbill—18 minutes behind Myron and
more than an hour behind Garnie. Until *all* the teams

have completed their required rest stops, it will be hard to tell exactly who is leading the race.

Now the long miles of autumn training pay off. The dogs have run 120 miles in less than 16 hours, have slept for only eight hours and are again moving down the trail at a brisk trot.

Evidently, though, it is not as brisk a trot as that of Angstman's team—I see his name on the Skyport Lodge sign-in sheet, next to the time: 9:37. I sign in at 10:20. Somewhere in that 41 miles we lost 20 minutes. I did stop for a short break and a chance to give the dogs a snack of beef liver at the halfway mark, but Angstman probably did something similar to that. His team is simply faster than mine. After five minutes, we head down the steep 11-mile trail that will bring us back to the level of Lake Superior in downtown Grand Marais.

Chiala comes into town riding in the basket of the sled. She has fallen down several times while making the descent from Skyport. She is one of the veterans of my team—the only one of my original dogteam that has made the transition to racing. Year by year, as the team has improved and she has grown older, it has become more difficult for her to keep up. Seeing her fall down and struggle to regain her footing tonight, I recall the night when, as a pup, she took that wild ride behind a runaway sled in Nemadji Forest. She has come a long way. Her Beargrease days are over. She gratefully flops down on her bed in the truck.

Duncan Storlie, my long-time mushing mentor, joins the race spectators at Grand Marais. I am happy to see him, since he is always full of serious advice, current statistics and quick humor. Tonight is no exception.

He draws me aside from the bustle around the team and gives me "the scoop" as he sees it: "Jamie is resting at Skyport; so is Linwood. Garnie and Angstman both blew through here within three minutes of each other, about 40 minutes ago. Jacobson can leave town at 12:59. My advice is to get this freight train out of here."

I listen and my resolve to take a two-hour rest here slowly evaporates. Third place. Forty minutes off the pace. It is hard to imagine settling in here for two full hours, in effect admitting that we cannot run with the leaders of the pack.

Somewhere inside me, the voice of reason and realism demands to be considered. I know, deep down, that I do not have a dogteam of the same depth and caliber as Angstman and Garnie. But it is the middle of the night, the turning point of the Beargrease, and my eagerness gets the best of me.

After a 40-minute delay, I sign out and the dogs trot up the hill again. Kazin, a rangy female from a sprint kennel, is limping slightly. I will have to drop her at Skyport. As I watch her troop up the hill I wonder if I have just made a bad decision.

There are rivalries in sled dog racing, as in all competitions. Small remarks along the trail and casual gestures can be taken by tired minds and turned into all manner of hidden meanings and ill will. Generally, though, the sport is pleasantly free from the cutthroat competition that occurs in some other professional athletics. Perhaps this is because, after all, the dogs are the athletes here.

The coaches can afford to be affable. Perhaps it is just too difficult to feel mean and nasty on a clear moonlit night, high on an open ridge, behind 14 trotting dogs. Still, as we climb toward Skyport, my thoughts run through the ranks of the competition and focus on several teams I would like to keep behind us.

Paul Fleming, the race's chief judge, meets us at Skyport. I like Paul. His mild, soft-spoken manner belies his insightful grasp of the race, the serious nature of the competition and his responsibility. As I remove Kazin from her harness, he comes over to mark her with a spray-painted X, denoting her withdrawal from the race. "This one doesn't want to play any more?"

It seems the perfect euphemism to me and I laugh. "Nope. She says she's had enough fun for one Beargrease."

In the Skyport checkpoint, my crew changes the runners on my sled. After the trip through the paved streets of Grand Marais, the smooth new polyethylene will make a noticeable difference.

Duncan and another friend work on lashing a makeshift brush bow into place on the front of the sled. Leaving Grand Marais, I slammed directly into a corner streetlight pole, shattering the laminated brush bow and probably waking some worthy citizens with my midnight tirade against downtown dog mushing.

Out of Skyport and down Devil's Track Lake, running a tenuous third in the race, I am watching dogs. Carefully, critically, my headlamp beam plays slowly up and down the team, pausing here and there to focus for a moment on a single swiftly moving leg or paw. Is D.J. limping now, there on the rear left? What about Fuji, is that bootie on her front right paw still in place? Is old Morris keeping his tugline tight? Up and down the team the questioning light moves. They look good, these 14. Maybe we did the right thing after all, pulling out of Grand Marais. Maybe they can hold it.

I am certain Jacobson will soon catch me and somewhere along the Bally Creek Road, he does. I see his light come bouncing up the trail behind me. I am stopped momentarily, putting a bootie on McDougal.

Robin, the defending champion of this race, goes quickly past, his team fresh after their eight-hour rest in Grand Marais. I try to count his dogs. It looks like he has ten. "How far ahead are those guys?" he asks.

"I don't know. I haven't seen them. Go get them."

"Okay. See you later."

I hope so, I think to myself. This is the longest stretch of this year's race course, 50 miles of hilly country ending at lake level again in the village of Tofte. Through the night we travel steadily and by dawn we are descending out of the hills. At 7:45 a.m. Friday, I sign into Tofte. Garnie, Angstman and Jacobson are there. My crew tells me that some of Myron's dogs are sick, with a flu or intestinal virus compounded by the stress of the race, and that Garnie is worried about his team as well. My entourage is on fire with the idea that I should take this chance to grab the lead.

But I have been behind these dogs all night. I know they are tired. We need two hours here, or three.

After an hour and forty-five minutes, I again succumb to temptation and we hit the trail, just behind Jacobson, in fourth position overall. There are 12 dogs in my team now—Morris and Henry seemed to be fading as we reached Tofte and I have dropped them.

By the time we climb back to the main trail along the ridgetop in the gradually warming sunshine, I realize the folly of my decision to leave Tofte so quickly.

On that 34 miles of trail between Tofte and Finland, the dogs pay for my mistakes. We have pushed too hard, too early. About ten miles out of Finland, Jake quits pulling and begins dragging on his neckline. I take his neckline off, he slows, drops back toward the sled, dodges the brush bow, falls over. I tuck him into the sled bag and he is sound asleep before we are moving again.

At Finland, I must face the consequences of my eagerness. The "pit crew" is standing by, ready to help us pass quickly through the checkpoint. I give them the word. "They're fried. We've got to stay here. I don't know how long it'll be. We just gotta stay here until they're a dogteam again."

Garnie, Angstman, Fiedler, Jacobson and Nelson are all out of Finland ahead of us, in that order. We leave, seven veteran dogs and I, after three hours and 20 minutes in the checkpoint. It is the long rest they have needed. They look much better. But the recovery has come at least one checkpoint too late.

My mood is grim. I kick myself mentally, over and over again. Don't you ever learn? Don't listen to the handlers. Don't look at the other teams. Just run your own race.

Now it is a matter of survival. I cannot push the team. They are too few and too near the quitting point. In a daze of disappointment and fatigue, I flip on my pocket tape player and it's Paul Simon: "Get these mutts away from me / you know / I don't find this stuff amusing any more. . . ."

No kidding.

In Beaver Bay, back at lake level again, we mushers are obliged to spend a moment at the gravesite of John Beargrease, the real, long-gone, Ojibway John Beargrease, for a simple remembrance ceremony. I stand there listening to the recitation by one of the checkpoint organizers and try again to imagine old John. Now my fancy nylon suit is coated with 50 hours of accumulated liver juice, whitefish broth and beaver grease, stained where I've spilled juice and coffee on it. My hair is crumpled and matted when I remove my grimy hat. It's getting easier to conjure up the old musher's image.

I feel surprisingly relaxed now. With seven dogs, I can take no chances. We are going to have to just hold it together all the way into Duluth. The racing, the pushing is over for us in this year's Beargrease.

Highway Two checkpoint, where we had been just two nights ago, is a long, mostly flat 36 miles from Beaver Bay. I sign in there at 3 a.m., Saturday morning, the fifth team to arrive. We have leapfrogged Robin again while he rested his team in Beaver Bay.

All the teams are required to take a four-hour rest at Highway Two, before heading for the finish line 47 miles away. It is a popular place for spectators to gather, since they are guaranteed a leisurely look at the teams. Tonight there is a roaring bonfire and a quiet group of people around it. The smells of jack pine smoke and cooking dog food fill the air. Over where the trail climbs out of the checkpoint, under some bright camera lights, Garnie and Angstman are leaving for Duluth, their layovers complete. They are now almost four hours ahead of me.

A long-distance race of sled dog teams is unique among sporting events. Here tonight, at Highway Two, deep in Minnesota's north woods, the atmosphere is hushed, expectant. The mood is more like that of a vigil than a race. There is a flurry of activity when a solitary team arrives or leaves, but most of the time it is quiet.

In a huge wall tent, heated by a barrel stove, a long row of cots has been set up for mushers and handlers desperately in need of a few hours of sleep. The air in there is thick with the smell of wood smoke, chili, spruce boughs, drying mukluk liners and the ever-present aroma of "dog." It is a far cry from the lights and hubbub of Ordean School on Wednesday evening.

After three hours of rest here, I begin to mull over a difficult decision. I ran seven dogs into this checkpoint and I need to run at least five across the finish line or be disqualified. Both Grayling and Tequila are tired. Do I dare run only five dogs out of here, leaving Tequila and Grayling behind? What if a dog among those five pulls up lame or simply quits between here and Duluth?

Then again, if I do take Grayling or Tequila or both of them, what will happen if I have to haul one of them in the sled with such a small team out front? The extra weight and effort of doing that could bring the remaining dogs to the point of mutiny. Weighing the alternatives, watching the dogs as we rub them down and talk cheerfully to them, I decide to go with five dogs. Let the chips fall where they may, I think to myself. We're just paying the price of blind ambition now.

At 7 a.m., my tiny team of five and I trot out of the Highway Two checkpoint. Banjo and Beaver are in lead, with Julie behind them and Brew and McDougal in wheel. All five of these dogs are capable of leading a team and all except McDougal have many years of racing behind them. Still, there will be no push for the finish, no kick. We are gliding. I feel like we are walking on eggs.

The day warms. The sun shines brightly. The dogs pant, but their gait stays smooth and steady. I feel like Beaver knows where we are—he has finished this race three times before, always in lead. The rest of the team looks steady and confident. Banjo is a veteran of at least five Iditarod Races and ran to Nome in Dean Osmar's winning 1984 team. It will take more than 50 miles of slow going to discourage her. Brew and McDougal, half brothers from a line of tough Inuit dogs, are what Rick Swenson might call "Rambo dogs." They seem to be all sinew and spring steel, even if a little short on brains.

And then there is Julie, a female originally from the kennel of George Attla in Alaska. She has been in full-blown estrus for the duration of the race. She is the oldest of these dogs, at nine years, and a veteran of years of sprint racing. Since the starting signal 62 hours ago her tugline has been tight whenever the team has been underway. If anything, she works *too* hard.

Robin Jacobson is behind us somewhere, having left Highway Two an hour and 19 minutes after we did. But my thoughts are not with him now, nor with any of the other teams. I just want these five dogs to cross the finish line in good form and for us all to put this race behind us and learn our lessons.

At the Idle Hour Restaurant we are nine miles from the finish line. We do not stop. There is no point in pausing here and no option of dropping any dogs from this team.

Someone hands me a can of soda as I run alongside the sled across the gravel parking area of the checkpoint. Nine miles to go. All downhill. We just might pull it off.

The trail begins to weave back and forth across small roads and ravines as we arrive on the outskirts of Duluth. The day has grown amazingly warm and sunny, perfect for spectators but hellishly hot for working dogs trained and accustomed to subzero cold. The team adopts that odd, mincing gait that I call "floating." Their feet hardly seem to touch the snow; their tuglines look as though they are made of elastic—tightening up, slacking off, again and again. It is a wonder that our combined efforts can keep the sled moving at all, even with a tiny load. But we move. Five miles to go.

Suddenly, it happens. Within a period of not more than ten seconds, I see Julie's gait wobble, become uncoordinated and in an instant she is down on the trail, flopped over on her side. I am seized by a mixture of panic, grief and compassion.

At that moment, there is no anger. Later I will be angry, but only at myself.

Quickly I stop the team, kick in the snowhook and rush forward. My first thought is that Julie is dead. But as I reach her I see her breathing, not gasping for breath, but simply lying there, her tongue partly out, looking up at me with a bewildered gaze.

I kneel beside her. We are on the shoulder of a wooded hillside, dropping toward another creek and bridge. Up ahead I see a road crossing and a man standing there in a safety-orange vest.

"You O.K. there, Jules? C'mon girl, we'll have a rest. That's it."

I ease her out of her neckline and take the toggle off her tugline. She feels limp, drained of strength and muscle tone. In the jargon of marathon runners, she has hit the wall and with a resounding crunch.

I carry her back to the sled and set her gently into the basket, covering her with the flap of the sled bag. I am fighting back tears of sadness, exhaustion and frustration. Julie closes her eyes, sighs deeply and falls asleep.

Four dogs. I have only four dogs. Over and over I imagine a horrible scene at the crowded finish line. Should I just call it quits here and send someone out with the truck? Disappear into the streets of Duluth and forget about limping over the finish line in disgrace?

No, you're tired. The dogs are tired. One thing at a time, I tell myself.

I reach the road crossing. I see that the man there is a ham radio operator, probably in touch with the people at the finish area. I stop the team.

"Can you radio ahead and tell them Dave Olesen has a dog in the basket that needs to be checked over by a vet? We're continuing down the trail."

"Will do. Uh, what's your dog's problem?"

"She's just plain tired, I think, but it could be something more than that. She just tipped right over. All right, you guys, let's go. Atta girl, Banj."

In the state of fatigue all mushers experience after too many sleepless hours, every emotion is magnified. The mental peaks and valleys are encountered in rapid succession, mile after mile, hour after hour. But now, there is no peak.

I feel saddened, sickened. An overreaction, I will be told. This is part of the game. In these middle-distance races you take them right to the edge. Sometimes they just can't do it.

At that moment, coming down the final hills toward Lester Park, with Julie sound asleep in the sled and four dogs in the team, I can't swallow those opinions. This, for me, is the worst imaginable situation. It is not good for sled dog racing and certainly not good for sled dogs, when four-dog teams walk to the finish line. Once again, I wrestle with the impulse to turn off into the woods and quit, right here.

"A mile to go. Way to go," people call out from the side of the trail.

A mile. "Julie, how you doin' there, Jules?" She looks up again. I stroke her behind the ears. The dogs out front glide along.

A quarter mile out, I can see the banner at the finish line. Judy Montgomery, the chief race veterinarian, is trotting alongside, saying, "I can't check her until you're across, Dave."

"Okay," I answer her. Then Kathy Anderson, the race director, is alongside, asking me what I'm going to do.

I decide to gamble. I will put Julie back into the team, giving me the required five dogs.

We pull up to the banner, with Beaver and Banjo nearly stepping on the official finish line and I set the snowhook. The dogs all turn toward me, perplexed. My face is contorted with emotion as I bend to lift Julie gently out of the sled.

I set her on her feet, fully expecting her to crumple into a heap.

She stands.

I pat her. "O.K., Julie girl, this is it."

We walk forward. I slip her neckline on again and put her toggle through the loop on her tugline.

"Just walk over the line, Jules, just walk over the line." I go back to the sled and pick up the hook. I am certain Julie is going to lie down the minute the team moves ahead.

"All right." The team, five tough, tired dogs, trots across the finish line. As a huge cheer goes up, Julie continues to stand there, her tugline tight, looking around.

It's over.

A few un-macho tears join the grape juice, soup and liver stains on the front of my numbered bib. I feel thoroughly undeserving of such animals as these.

At the mandatory meeting before the race, Paul Fleming had gone through the rules, one by one, with all the mushers and their crews. In closing, he had said, slightly tongue-in-cheek, "Well, let's have a good dog race. Run 'em 'til they drop."

Julie has just gone him one better.

We finished fifth in the race, for the second year in a row. Our total time for the 368 miles was 67 hours, 43 minutes, 51 seconds. Myron Angstman edged out Joe

Garnie in the final stretch, finishing first in 63:09:36, a new course record.

The veterinarians checked my team at the finish line, concentrating on Julie. She was deemed to be all right and her dramatic collapse was attributed to simple fatigue, "hitting the wall," compounded by the fact that she was in estrus. She was and is one of those rare dogs for whom there is no *gradual* slacking off—they pull hard until they cannot pull any longer; they run until their physical reserves are gone.

By the next morning, Julie was jumping happily around the dog truck with the rest of the team, flirting with her suitors and being bred by Tom, much to my dismay. With her pregnancy, her racing season was over.

Julie was not with us on the 1987 Iditarod Trail and she has not run in any long-distance race since her first and last Beargrease.

ON THE ROAD

W**E WERE GOING ONLY ABOUT 30 MILES AN HOUR.**
The road, Manitoba Highway Six, 300 miles north of
Winnipeg, consisted of a single pair of tracks from the
tires of a semi-trailer somewhere ahead of us. "Break-
away traffic all the way to Ponton" someone had announced on the C.B. radio.

"We" were a 1972 Ford three-quarter-ton pickup
towing a trailer. The trailer was loaded with 1,000
pounds of dog food and the truck itself was filled to
overflowing with 19 dogs, two sleds, a three-wheeled
training cart, winter camping gear for a month, all of
our tools and clothing. There was Mike Dietzman, dozing, crumpled in the far corner of the cab and myself
behind the wheel.

The air was thick with wet autumn snow and a skim
of ice covered the pavement. The truck's heater was broken. The cab floor was so rusted away that it consisted
almost entirely of ancient foam sleeping pads, newspa-
pers, Fritos bags and old pastry wrappers from the Barbara
Ann Bakery in Ely, Minnesota. It was 1 a.m., the second

night of November. We were on the road, but not for long.

"Here we go."

"Huh?"

"We're hitting the ditch."

"HUH?"

Whatever started the swerving fishtail motion of the trailer, probably a chance combination of steering, wind and ice, did not seem like a force with which a driver could argue. Like a true subarctic Taoist, I opted to go with the flow. In this case, truck, trailer, gear, dogs, mushers and pastry wrappers all flowed gracefully over the highway's left shoulder, down an embankment and came to a stop in a level ditch, a foot deep in snow.

"Well, Mikey, I think it's bedtime."

"What the ... where the ... how ... aw, geez."

"Just lost it. Period. Time for bed. Hey, we're out of everybody's way, right? Those truckers can just keep on playing 'break-away traffic' all night, whatever the hell that means. I've had it."

The dogs were already fed and had been let down from their boxes back in Grand Rapids. We dug out our sleeping bags, laid out a tarp and a pair of foam pads and settled in for the night. Just as we were both plummeting into sweet unconsciousness, a diesel throbbed toward us, its halogen fog lights picked us out in the ditch and the rig throttled back, shifting gears. It took him most of a mile to stop. Shivering in my long underwear, I climbed up to the door of our truck, turned the ignition key and switched on the C.B.

"Break for that southbound rig, this is the ditch."

"Yeah, go ahead there, ditch."

"Well, we're just gonna camp here and deal with this mess in the morning. Thanks for stopping."

"Yeah, okay. The plow from Wabowden is broke down, eh? So I don't know when they'll get this scraped off for you."

"Okay then. Thanks. G'night."

"Righto." His diesel roared again and the running lights on the rear of his trailer dwindled into the snowstorm. I returned to my sleeping bag, thoroughly chilled.

"Are we having fun yet?" Mike asked from the depths of his goose-down cocoon.

"Yeah, I think it's just starting. You have to be patient. You don't want to be greedy about this stuff."

Seven hours later, the sky was beginning to brighten. We climbed out of our sacks, dressed and dropped the dogs around the truck. They stretched and nipped at each other, pissed and scratched and generally made it clear that they thought this snow-filled ditch was a fine spot for a break.

We left them out while with a shovel and our boots we began to clear a path back up the sloping shoulder and onto the road. It was about a four-foot total rise back to road level. After the night's storm, the road was coated with hard black ice beneath six inches of fresh snow. Another trucker pulled over while we shoveled and scraped; he surveyed our situation and decided that there was no way he could get enough traction to tug out our load.

"The plow at Wabowden is broke down, eh?"

"Yeah, we know. Thanks. We'll figure something out."

"So . . . like . . . where are you guys *going?*"

"Leaf Rapids. We're dog racers."

"Oh." He said it as if no further explanation of either our predicament or our sanity was needed, jumped up into his cab and crept away in compound low. We finished clearing our long, angled path up to the road and put the dogs back in the truck.

I climbed in and turned the key. The engine cranked eagerly but would not fire. Again and again I turned it over with no result, until I feared for the life of the battery. If we dribbled gas directly into the carburetor, the engine would catch, then die. I took out the fuel filter, blew it clean and then started to work on the most likely culprit: the valve in the fuel system where gas from the auxiliary tank joined the main fuel line. In a dog food pan I lit a few briquets of charcoal and when they were glowing I propped them gingerly up under the valve.

"You gonna torch it?"

"Yeah, gotta cut down on roadside litter. Get the dogs and gear out. When it blows we'll just sled out of here."

"You very funny man."

"Tanks."

The thawing of the valve did the trick and the truck roared to life. I gently let out the clutch and punched the accelerator. The rear wheels spun wildly. The truck and trailer didn't budge.

Above the clatter—about six of the engine's eight cylinders were firing—we considered our options and decided to use our ace in the hole: the dogs. We laid out a long gangline, with space for 16 dogs. Makepeace, Christie and Chiala would stay in their boxes. We laid out harnesses for everyone and led the team into position one by one. With the 16 hooked up, all of them screaming at this first chance to run in several days, Mike went out in front of the leaders and I got behind the wheel.

After checking for traffic, only a formality on this road, he gave me the signal. I shouted to the team, gunned the engine, the dogs slammed into their tugs and the whole works—dogs, truck and trailer, churned up onto Highway Six again.

Shouting and laughing, we guided the entire 90-foot parade off to the road's edge and began to dismantle our portable winch. When dogs, lines and harnesses were all stowed back in their boxes, we lurched ahead toward Ponton, Thompson and the Churchill River.

About four miles along, we eased to a nerve-wracking stop as ten woodland caribou trotted down the invisible center line of the highway, then split into two groups and turned off into the spruce woods on each side.

The tension of the past night began to dissolve. We were in the North again. On the road. And having fun.

Traveling with a team of dogs and a truckload of gear, in midwinter, on the remote highways of northern North America can have its memorable moments. Considering the fact that dog mushers tend to place a much higher value on fast and trustworthy huskies than on fast and trustworthy vehicles, the ingredients for automotive epics are all there—worn-out trucks, old tires, heavy loads, snowstorms, bitter cold, long nights and endless miles of empty white highway. Compound this with the presence of an urgent schedule to meet, be it the start of a race or the beginning of an expedition, and the plot rapidly thickens.

The best advice I've ever received on mechanized dogteam transport came from my friend, Arleigh Jorgenson, on the morning of our departure for five weeks of traveling and racing. This was to culminate with our arrival in Yellowknife, 3,000 meandering miles away. As he hoisted the 20th of 29 dogs into its box aboard the flatbed of his aging pickup, I stooped to check the truck's sagging leaf springs. Arleigh smiled an old-veteran sort of smile: "You're okay until the springs start to bend *downward.*" He paused, sensing that I was unconvinced. "You know, you can't *think* about all this too much; you just have to *do* it."

I nodded. We continued loading dogs, not thinking, just doing. Twenty-seven, twenty-eight, twenty-nine. . . Moments later, the truck swayed ponderously down the gravel lane from my dog yard, turned northwest and we began an unlikely odyssey that was to use up five tires. Over 6,000 miles, five weeks, four races and many sleepless nights. It was to be my initiation into dog-truck expeditioning.

I had driven north with dogs prior to that, but never with two full teams, an ambitious itinerary and so little pocket money. Before I ever owned a proper dog box with individual boxes for each dog, my teams and I had logged many miles on northern highways. On those first trips, the dogs rode together right in the bed of the pickup, through the dust and heat and flies of summer and the dark and snow and cold of winter. But this time we had a traveling kennel and we were going racing. Our winnings would go directly into the gas tank. We would stay with other mushers all over the north, train our teams along the way and truly depend upon our dogs' performance to get us down the road. I thought it would all be so adventurous. It was. And it wasn't.

"What you got in the boxes—chickens?"

"Nope. Dogs."

"Dogs! Sleigh dogs? Geez, those boxes are kinda small, don't you think?"

Okay. At this point something has to be said on behalf of traveling dog mushers everywhere. We depend on our dogs as athletes. We take care of them night and day, all year long. We train them and coddle them and feed them and water them, religiously. Why would we cram them into boxes that were too small, boxes in which they could not ride comfortably for days and weeks and months at a time, being let down and taken care of on a strict regimen?

Watch the dogs. Watch them jump up *into* their boxes, turn around, look out, smiling (dogs do smile) and lie down, happy to be home. Why would a musher put so much effort into a dogteam and then truck them around the continent in boxes that were *too small*?

Yet at every gas station, here come Mr. and Mrs. Chevy Blazer and their overstuffed seat-cushion of a schnauzer, gawking and moaning, "Ohhh, the poor things." While the bleary-eyed musher, who has just driven all night, stopping three times on some godforsaken stretch of highway at 5,000 below zero to feed or water or simply exercise his or her dogs, is expected to suddenly see the light and realize, after all these years, that, "Hey, you're right, mister; these things *are* too small. I better stop right here in the middle of Saskatchewan and build myself a new dog box, so my 50-pound racing huskies can play volleyball in there while we gas up."

I have heard that there are dog mushers, sprint drivers mostly, who launch off down the highway in shiny, perfectly maintained trucks, carrying loads well within the sensible range suggested by the manufacturer, on good tires, with heaters and gauges that work, their pockets overflowing with credit cards, traveler's checks and cold hard cash. That's what I've *heard*.

What I've seen, first-hand, are aspiring long-distance mushers bound for the Iditarod Trail or the Yukon Quest or the Beargrease or some other race, with 500 pounds of frozen beaver meat and ground chicken fat, half a ton of dry dog food, 22 dogs, four sleds, a bald spare tire, 1,200 dog booties, three cassette tapes and a Walkman, two toolboxes, six pints of gas line antifreeze, a bag of doughnuts just coming up on 1,300 miles and enough cash to get them barely beyond either the Alaska, Minnesota, or Northwest Territories borders. Call it a warped perspective. Call it a separate reality.

It is separate. And it is, without a doubt, reality. When a tire goes flat on a long downhill grade just short of the Liard River on the Alaska Highway at 2 a.m., at −20 degrees and both spares are already mounted on the truck and rolling down the road, reality of at least one variety looms just ahead. You take your foot off the gas, ease the hissing front right tire over onto the snow-covered shoulder as far as you dare and gently apply the brakes.

"I can't believe it," says Kristen from the other side of the cab. "Do you know that until we left on this trip I had never, not once in my entire life, had a flat tire?"

This being the journey's third flat tire in as many days, you're not sure what is the best response to her statement. Maybe unfounded optimism is in order. "Well, the hot springs are just up ahead. There's a roadhouse there. We can get the tire fixed, walk it back here, put it on and camp at the springs. It'll be nice."

So you do. And, surprisingly, it is. And the next night you're in Watson Lake, Yukon Territory, where you get a good deal on two brand-new tires and three days later you're in Knik, Alaska, getting food drop supplies ready for the Iditarod Race. The truck is parked, the dogs are out on a training run, the leaf springs are bending upward again and all's right with the world.

Perhaps these driving epics are linked to the same mental aberrations that cause long-distance dog mushers to aspire to such a life in the first place. For whatever reason, it seems that we all invariably drive nonstop, or as close to nonstop as we can when carrying dozens of dogs and confronting the vagaries of machinery and weather. Motels are expensive. Roadside camping in midwinter is no picnic. It makes more sense, to the mind of a dog musher, to *just keep driving*. This way of traveling is efficient in the same way a river barge is efficient—slowly and steadily—but it is not very often fun. A person tends to wake up at 4:30 a.m. in a dark truck, windows frosted on the inside, for a sparkling bit of conversation:

"Uh. . ."

"What time did you pull over?"

"Mmm. I don't know. 3:15, I guess."

"Oh. Where are we?"

"I think we're just south of Steen River."

"Huh."

Yawn.

"Well, they'll be open in a couple hours. We'll need to get some gas, right?"

"Nah, there's still some in the jug, up top. We can go to Enterprise."

"O.K. I'll drop the dogs. They went in at 9:30, didn't they?"

"Yeah, I guess."

Out the door, cold and clear. The Mackenzie Highway, northern Alberta. Four hundred fifty miles to Yellowknife. Pull out the cables, clip them to the truck bumpers, let out the dogs. Talk to them, scratch a few ears. Climb up on the roof of the truck and untie the red five-gallon jug of gas. Hop down, pour it into the tank. Lift each dog back up into its box. Tie up the gas jug again. Put away the tie-out cable. Scrape the frost off the inside of the windshield. Write down the odometer mileage and "5 gals.," because the gas gauge doesn't work. Find the thermos. Pour a cup of lukewarm coffee. Pull out the tape player and the earphones. Put in Joni Mitchell. Start the engine. Turn on the headlights. Rollin'.

"If we get to Fort Rae in daylight, we should run these guys there."

"Yeah."

"Wake me up if you get tired."

"You bet."

Peg the speedometer at fifty-five. Switch on Joni. Think about whether to make a longer gangline for the Yellowknife race and whether $500 for eighth place will pay half the expenses on the trip home. Assuming you can finish *that* well. "Wild things run fast. . ." sings Ms. Mitchell.

There are, of course, ways other than trucks to move dogteams around the continent and beyond. I remember vividly an evening on the train between Churchill and Thompson, Manitoba, bound south with Will Steger after a six-week trip up the west coast of Hudson's Bay. The dogs were housed in separate small wooden crates (not *too* small, mind you) and together with them we were rattling along in the baggage car, watching the spring twilight of the taiga roll by outside the huge open doors. For our senses, long limited to the sterile world of the pack ice and winter tundra, the sudden warmth of May, the greenery, the returning geese and ducks and the moist air made a banquet and the mingled smells of dogs and train and boreal forest were nothing short of intoxicating. We leaned on each side of the open door, silent, breathing deeply. The train eased to a stop along a deserted stretch of track, for no apparent reason.

Out in the tangle of black spruce that bordered the grade, we saw them. A male and a female lynx, sitting together on a sedge-covered hummock, seemingly unaware of the train and of us. They tipped their heads back one at a time, as if wailing, but any sound was smothered by the rumble of the locomotive. Gradually they seemed to become aware of us and moved slowly away, huge paws padding on moss, their movement fluid and controlled, as if the effort of walking took only a tiny fraction of the speed and energy contained within them.

The train banged and creaked into motion again and we stood, transfixed, for another hour or more, until the brief hours of near-darkness began. Windburned, slightly frostbitten, smiling, rolling home.

The next year, also in early May, I loaded seven dogs into the empty hold of a DC-3, bound south across Great Slave Lake from Yellowknife to Hay River. I was alone with the dogs, my partners having already returned south to jobs and families. Our truck had been driven to Winnipeg six weeks earlier, in anticipation of our return from Baker Lake. But we had not completed our planned crossing of the barrenlands.

Deep snow and our own lack of experience had forced us to backtrack from the Thelon River to Reliance and we caught a flight to Yellowknife on a passing Twin Otter. Stepping out of that plane, we were greeted by the news that the Mackenzie River ice road was closed for the season—there would be no way to drive the truck to Yellowknife for several weeks.

Inquiring around the airport, I arranged a ride in a DC-3 that evening. The trip would be completely unofficial and completely free of charge. At the appointed time I met the pilot on the tarmac and began loading the dogs into the plane. I had no boxes for them, but they all behaved well until the start of our takeoff roll.

The noise and sudden acceleration caused panic in the jumble of overheated, nervous dogs and before long a huge fight was in progress. The pilot glanced back as we climbed to cruising altitude to see me in the midst of a pile of snarling, bleeding, yelping huskies. Perhaps fearing a hijack attempt once the team had finished with me, he reached back and pulled the cockpit door closed behind him. After ten minutes order had been restored, the worst offenders were tied in opposite corners of the fuselage and the pilot took a peek back once again: "You all right?"

I assured him I was and soon we landed in the midst of a driving rainstorm in Hay River. Soaking wet, my face peeling with sun- and windburn, my wool trail clothes torn and covered with dog hair and dog blood, knowing not a soul in town at that moment, I felt thoroughly undeserving of my fate. But we were south of the lake, south of the Mackenzie and heading home again.

Three days later, still looking like something any decent cat would refuse to drag in, the dogs and I were basking in 70-degree sunshine amidst the bustle of downtown Edmonton. The dogs' crates had come from Winnipeg and we would be eastbound on the next train. The Thelon River, the barrenlands, sleds and tents and skis—they all seemed to belong on another planet. I sat on the green sod outside the train station, scratching Sinker behind the ears and trying to avoid the curious stares of passing secretaries, accountants and bureaucrats.

Another two days and we were back in the '67 Chevy pickup, rolling alongside the Rainy River. On the road, yet again.

Trucks, trains, planes . . . and boats. In the summer of 1983, Mitch Gilbert and I hauled an old wooden Thompson runabout up to Yellowknife, with my ten dogs along for the ride, and motored south out of Yellowknife Bay at midnight on July 3. We spent the summer at the far east end of Great Slave Lake, with the dogs running free on an island while we camped across the cove from them. We took turns looking after the team and making solo forays into the country nearby. Finally, in mid-September, having been unable to arrange purchase of what later became my homestead, we loaded the ten dogs and our gear back in the boat and steered for Yellowknife, 250 miles away.

Two weeks later we arrived, the dogs strewn across the deck of the freighter *Hearne Channel,* our runabout and its broken-down outboard motor in tow behind us. Luckily, we had met a party of prospectors staking claims near McKinley Point, worked for them for a day and accepted the offer of a ride back to town aboard their boat. The dogs seemed to take well to boat travel. I have heard of a team or two along the Yukon River that spend entire summers aboard river barges.

A modern dogteam, especially one involved in long expeditions or competition, must adapt to many kinds of travel. It is a credit to these dogs, as essentially tied to wild country and Arctic expanses as they are, that they can adapt so completely and happily to all of our modern methods of moving them from place to place.

I honestly think the dogs enjoy traveling, the experience of strange sights and sounds and—of the most significance to them—exotic odors never encountered along the home trails. They show their toughness, adaptability and nearly constant good natures as they are loaded, crated, checked through baggage departments, exercised at train stations, picketed on airport fences and crammed together on the decks of storm-tossed boats.

But it is the road, the old pickup truck with the dogs in their boxes on the back, the dark snowy miles and the pleasant late-night glare of Canadian truck stops, that we mushers know best.

In a dream world, all dog trucks would be new and well maintained. All mushers would fly to distant races on jet airliners, rent late-model trucks with freshly painted kennels, win the races, collect their generous purse money and wing back to their homesteads along the northern fringe. But until then, for most of us, there will be the road and life in the not-so-fast lane.

It's evening on the Cross Lake Reserve, a Cree community in northern Manitoba. The dog trucks are pulling into town for the weekend race. Old Horace Halcrow greets each arriving musher in his simple, government-issue house, a turned-up cap above his broad smile. He knows exactly what we want—a place to drop our dogs, warm water to soak their food, a cup of coffee and a place to throw a sleeping bag.

We greet the other drivers, familiar faces with fast dogteams. We will not win *this* race.

Talk turns nervously to the purse money, the prospect of reduced prizes, problems within the race organization. The length of the trail is always a concern, since here it sometimes turns out to be much shorter than expected. Arleigh and I consider our teams for the race, talk briefly of joining forces and decide against it. There will be enough money for everyone finishing the three days of the race, enough to get us down the road and on to Fort Rae in the Northwest Territories.

The dog's food is ready. We go out to the truck and let the teams down. The jangle of short tie-out chains against the bumpers, the rich smells of cooked beaver meat and crusty chore gloves, laughter from a cluster of young boys along the town's main street. Another stop along the road.

THE LONGEST NIGHT

I KNEW THAT THE FRIENDLY MAN IN THE WHITE MASK
and gown and the pale blue surgeon's cap was only mark-
ing time, waiting for my lights to go out. He sat alongside
me under the bright glare of huge fluorescent bulbs. He
had just eased an intravenous needle into my forearm and
had then placed a plastic mask over my mouth and nose.
Now he was rambling on about Quetico Provincial Park,
canoeing and how he thought it sounded fascinating to
travel there in winter, by dogteam.

I nodded slightly and my head seemed to roll wildly
with the motion. Curious, I flexed my fingers. They re-
sponded, but my mental commands to them were faltering. I was falling . . . asleep. . . .

McKellar Hospital, Thunder Bay, Ontario, about
noon on the 17th of February, 1982. At 10 a.m., I had
been on the south end of Kashahpiwi Lake, over a
hundred miles southwest of Thunder Bay, in a white
canvas wall tent with a snow floor and a wood-burning
Yukon stove. My fever had gone down and I had felt
reasonably normal except for the hot coal that seemed

to have lodged in the lower right quadrant of my abdomen. It had been a long, strange, delirious night.

It was supposed to have been a vacation. Six friends, ten dogs, a week in the winter wilds of Quetico Park north of Ely, Minnesota, and south of Atikokan, Ontario. Like all serious modern expeditions, we had required an acronym—some catchy set of initials which would epitomize the spirit of our adventure and our deep-rooted goals. Winter Expedition Into Remote Districts filled the bill perfectly—WEIRD. Given the group's ragtag background, a decidedly countercultural bias and our common suspicion of lofty expeditionary ideals, the tongue-in-cheek spirit of WEIRD caught on quickly. Duncan designed a WEIRD banner, which he proudly unfurled every morning and evening on the tent pole to the accompaniment of raucous blues riffs on his kazoo. Dave Bryce had brought WEIRD T-shirts, which looked sensational on Beck and Pierre, his wheel dogs—especially when combined with sunglasses and baseball caps.

There was a more-than-medicinal supply of 151-proof Arctic Snakebite Medicine in our sled loads and the conversation on the trail and around camp was so convoluted and sarcastic that a stranger would have thought us all completely warped. We were out to enjoy ourselves, to take a holiday in wild, empty country in midwinter, with experienced companions, no strict agenda and two good teams of dogs.

We set out on a Sunday morning from a cabin just east of Ely and camped that night just across the international border at Ottawa Island. The next day, we mushed and skied and laughed our way up to the north arm of Basswood Lake. That night, the standard voyageur concoction *soupe aux pois,* split pea soup, was on the menu. This seemed to me to be a particularly volatile batch, chased as it was by rum and some horrendous instant butterscotch pudding. So when nature demanded that I exit the tent at 4 a.m. I attributed it to indigestion and when my gut still ached and rumbled through the following morning on the trail I did not think much of it.

By noon and our stop for lunch, I sensed that there might be something seriously wrong with my insides. Occasional sharp bursts of pain shot through my abdomen, punctuating a constant twisting ache. I switched places with one of the day's mushers and the break from skiing and carrying a pack helped to moderate the pain. By late afternoon, though, I had that feeling of slight detachment that fever brings. My gut ache was the worst I had ever had and I was thinking I had better turn back toward Ely and the roadhead while daylight remained. When a moose crossed the swamp ahead of us on the portage into Kashahpiwi Lake, the dogs sprinted ahead. As I heaved to tip the sled over and stop the team, the wave of pain and delirium that swept over me nearly laid me out in the snow. WEIRD was getting weird.

At the south end of Kashahpiwi, a long lake edged by tall granite cliffs, we stopped to camp for the night. While my companions set up the tent and stove, cut firewood and picketed the dogs, I lay in a sleeping bag. I knew by then that I was seriously ill, more ill than I had ever been. Ever ready to assume the worst in such situations, I mused somewhat surreally on whether this spot, on this bright winter afternoon, was a good place to die. I decided that the setting would suffice and at the same time made up my mind to go down kicking and clawing.

The tent was pitched and I was helped into it. One of the WEIRD team, Dave Bryce, is a physician who was then living near Bemidji, Minnesota, with his family and a team of dogs. He joined me in the tent, hustled everyone else out the door and gave me a thorough physical examination. After writing down his findings and what I could tell him about the onset of the illness, he called the group back into the tent.

He waited until everyone was sitting or kneeling on the tent's floor and began. "It's pretty clear that Ole has an acute abdomen."

Duncan couldn't resist. "Yeah, I'd heard rumors he had a cute little something-or-other. . ." Everyone laughed nervously and I told Dunc that *he* was a sick man.

"This is serious," Bryce continued tersely. "I think it's appendicitis. He needs to be operated on. We've got to make some decisions."

The biggest decision the group faced was obvious: whether to bring me out to the roadhead by dogteam, or to send word out and bring help, in the form of an aircraft, back to our camp. We had only the dogs, our skis, our combined experience and Bryce's medical expertise to rely on. We had no radio, no emergency beacon and we were in an area rarely traversed by aircraft in winter. It was nearly certain that there was no other party of travelers between us and the roadhead, nearly 40 miles away and—given the designated wilderness status of the park and the boundary waters—any other group would have been at no mechanical advantage to us.

Here, I think, it is time for a digression. For beyond the somewhat cliché and heroic circumstances that we found ourselves in that evening, there are some controversial issues. The bizarre modern combinations of legislated wilderness, jet helicopters, emergency communications and night-long runs by dogteam raise some thorny questions.

We face, by design or default, the possibility of such emergencies whenever we travel into remote country by any means. When we deliberately choose to travel by nonmechanized, slow, quiet means, we leave behind some of the options of quick response. When, for reasons of budget or philosophy or practicality, we go without high-tech means of communication, we again make a choice that limits our response in case of injury or illness.

The cynics, the ever-practical, modern techno-philes, would have had a glorious evening with us on Kashahpiwi Lake.

"See?" they would have smiled. "You go chasing off by dogsled into some fairy-tale wilderness, but as soon as something goes wrong you pull out the stops and demand the best that technology can offer."

They would then have launched into a long discourse on our basic irresponsibility, how confused our logic and values were and how, if we wanted to live like the old-timers, perhaps we had better just be prepared to die like them also.

I tire of these people and of their outlook. Much of what they say, of course, is valid and cannot be ignored. We do seek what is now something of a contrived detachment when we travel by dogteam, or canoe, or on foot, in areas designated as "wilderness." And we do, when catastrophe strikes, reach almost instinctively for help in whatever swift modern form we can find it.

Within the arguments of these people against such "double standards," I perceive something mean, some streak of longing that we *will*, finally, get what's coming to us Out There and prove them right. It is as if they want wild country to bear out their perception of it as a treacherous, constantly antagonistic environment that is eager, in fact *scheming,* to swallow up those foolish enough to travel it without the latest technological whiz-toys.

In response, I must admit, a similar perverse wish rises within me—to see these perpetual doomsayers, a whole herd of them, armed with all the latest insulating, pacifying, communicating safeguards, swallowed up completely, their technology grounded and ineffectual, the wild, unavoidable otherside of the landscape asserting itself over them *and* their puny protections. For there are still, in the earth's wild corners, combinations of misfortune and circumstance that are insurmountable.

There was no philosophizing in the darkening tent that evening. We were facing facts, measuring odds and considering options. After a sum total of decades of experience in *simulating* such wilderness emergencies in our work as guides and outdoor teachers, our group was facing the real thing.

I was sick and getting sicker. It was nearly dark and getting darker. We had no radio, no snowmobile. No one would be checking up on us.

Though all of us in the group, except perhaps myself, could quite deservedly have assumed the role of leader that night, it was Duncan who gradually took charge. Calm, always methodical and now completely serious, he led the discussion and the planning that it generated.

We decided we would send word out, that night, by dogteam.

The risks of waiting until morning, or of having me ride on a sled, were too great. Mitch Gilbert and Will Hauser would travel together with eight dogs, directly back the way we had come, to the Fall Lake Road, east of Ely. There they would make contact by phone with officials in both Ontario and Minnesota and arrange an immediate evacuation by whatever means possible.

"We need to write everything down right now, step by step," said Dunc. "You don't want to try to think of all this stuff after you've been running dogs and skiing all night."

One by one, items of equipment and backup plans and specific details were recorded in duplicate by Mitch and Willy. About an hour after we had convened in the tent, everyone except myself was scurrying around the camp, packing the sled, waxing skis, checking flashlights and laying out dog harnesses.

In 1982, none of us in that group had much experience with running dogs at night. None of us even owned a headlamp. The regimen of running and resting and feeding snacks to the team for maximum efficiency was unknown to us. When we ran teams at night, it was always on familiar routes for short errands.

The dogs, too, lacked the experience that my team has now gained from several seasons of long distance racing. When they arrived in camp at the end of a day of slow, steady travel, they were fed and picketed on a tie-out cable and they quickly settled in for 12 to 15 hours of sleep. Tonight, they would instead be expected to work—in fact, to race.

At 10 p.m. Mitch stuck his head in through the tent flap and announced that he and Willy were taking off. Bryce had just given me my second of five successive doses of Keflex, a powerful antibiotic. He had also prescribed, in all seriousness, a stiff shot of overproof rum. My fever was high and rising. I remember Mitch talking, us wishing each other well and the noise of dogs being harnessed.

Evidently there was a brief dog fight 50 yards down the trail and a big male dog of Dave's, Niki, was removed from the team as a precaution. This left the messengers with seven dogs. Their leader was Mukluk, a feisty little female known more for her inconsistency than her talents. When she was "on" she was second to none as an open-terrain command leader. When she was "off," though, a musher ended up doing her work for her, out at the head of the team, mile after tedious mile.

The night must have been a long one on the trail. The route south led through small lakes and portages to Basswood Lake; the trail was punchy and narrow. There were several stretches of thin creek ice to negotiate near Isabella Creek. Across Basswood the wind had obliterated all but a few traces of our tracks from two days before. Mitch has always been taciturn and meticulous under pressure and I gathered from later conversations that there were a few tense moments between him and Willy in those 30-odd miles. By about 5 a.m., they had reached the south end of Hoist Bay on Basswood. At that point Mitch and the dogs went on ahead for the final eight-mile run to Fall Lake. Both men were back in familiar country by then and Willy, who had spent the entire night on skis, had begun to tire.

Evidently, it was a good night for Mukluk. Mitch recalled later that he was able to direct her across Basswood by a combination of spoken commands and guidance from a flashlight's dimming beam. Most of the time, though, she seemed to follow the trail precisely without help, using her nose and perhaps her feet to find it beneath the drifted snow.

In the tent on Kashahpiwi, I was pampered and attended to as I slipped in and out of a fog of feverish dreams and brief, intense waves of pain. The fire was kept stoked. Bryce monitored my temperature, signs and symptoms. Both Duncan and Joe Sjostrom were at work outside, bucking firewood and stamping a huge SOS symbol into the snow. There was speculation about the success of the trip out to the roadhead and about what time help might arrive. There was also growing concern about the weather, but to this I was oblivious.

The WEIRD trip had been sunny and pleasant for its first two days, but that evening the temperature climbed into the 30s, thick clouds moved in and there was so much moisture in the air that rain seemed imminent. For fixed-wing aircraft, bush planes of the sort that could land on Kashahpiwi, freezing rain was impossible flying weather. The surface of the plane would quickly become loaded with ice and the lifting power of the wings would be destroyed. If freezing rain began, evacuation by air would be out of the question until it ended.

Mitch and the seven dogs reached the end of the Fall Lake road at about 7 a.m. Wednesday morning. He immediately began making phone calls to try to organize a rescue. Since our camp was across the international border in Ontario and since the weather in Ely had already deteriorated to the point where airplane flight was unthinkable, his efforts centered on getting word to the

Canadian authorities in Atikokan. From there word went to Sioux Lookout, Ontario, where it reached a provincial air ambulance helicopter, "Bandage One." Its crew decided to attempt an immediate flight to Kashahpiwi Lake despite the dismal weather forecast for the area.

I was sitting up in my sleeping bag, resting against a packsack, writing in my journal, when we heard the rotors and turbine of the chopper approaching from the north. With dawn had come a lessening of my fever; probably the inflammation of my appendix had been cooled considerably by the huge doses of Keflex. I actually had begun to wonder whether my friends and the incoming helicopter crew had worked for nothing—perhaps I did not have appendicitis after all. But through the night, Dr. Bryce had been thoroughly convinced of his initial diagnosis. Now that help had arrived, the assurance that I *did* have a very serious illness was oddly welcome.

It was 10 a.m., exactly 12 hours since the dogteam had pulled out of camp, when the big Bell helicopter settled down directly in the center of the stamped-out SOS. Jumpsuited paramedics scrambled out and in a moment Bryce was poking an intravenous needle into my forearm and kidding me about having flaccid veins. I was lifted onto a stretcher, hustled through the wide door in the chopper's hull and the stretcher and I were strapped in place.

I caught a brief glimpse of Dunc, Joe and Dave standing near the big white tent just as the rotor wash from our takeoff flattened it. Through headphones and an intercom, I answered the paramedic's questions and asked her how fast the helicopter cruised. "About 180 miles an hour," she said. "We should be landing in Thunder Bay in about 35 minutes." As we talked, Willy Hauser was just reaching the Fall Lake Road after 40 miles on skis. He headed into Ely in search of Mitch, some breakfast and a bed, perhaps not in that order.

After our landing at the Thunder Bay airport, I was transferred from "Bandage One" to an ordinary four-wheeled ambulance. We drove quickly to McKellar Hospital minus siren and lights and checked in through the emergency room. Suddenly awash in bright white light and surrounded by clean-scrubbed orderlies, I was keenly aware of my trail clothes and their pungent smells of spruce smoke, sled dog and sweat. I chuckled as I thought of the old adage about wearing clean underwear every day in case of just such a situation. The attendants did not seem flustered by my aroma, though, as I was stripped and helped into a clean gown. A doctor and the surgeon each examined me. I was scrubbed and shaved for surgery and wheeled to the room where the talkative anesthesiologist put me under.

"A routine appendectomy" was how the surgeon described the operation when he visited me the next day, adding that mine was about the "hottest" appendix he had ever removed. Evidently help and surgery had come just in time. Three days later, as the WEIRD crew straggled in from Quetico Park to Fall Lake, I was out of the hospital and shuffling painfully around the bus station in Duluth, Minnesota. That night, we were all together again for dinner in Ely and the bantering and humor had resumed.

"I swear some people will do anything to get out of their night for dishwashing. . . ."

The whole event lends itself to some romanticizing. "Sled dogs save stricken musher" is a catchy phrase, but in fact it was modern surgery and a jet helicopter that finally tipped the scales in my favor. Yet even the cynics, always ready to shake their heads over our fairy-tale pursuit of dog mushing, cannot ignore the facts. We had been on Kashahpiwi Lake. I had been very sick. Mitch and Willy, the crew in camp and seven dogs together made possible the rescue that may well have saved my life.

Mukluk, with her one blue eye and one brown eye and one good nose, led the way to a telephone. The freezing rain held off just long enough to allow the helicopter flight and I'm here to tell the story. Other mushers, trappers, woodsmen and hunters all over the North, over the years, alone and distant in their camps and cabins, have not been so lucky.

Thanks, Muk. Thanks, WEIRDos. Thanks, Bandage One.

Iditarod Route
Anchorage to Nome

A ROOKIE'S IDITAROD

IN MID-NOVEMBER, 1985, WALKING ALONG THE ROAD into the town of Leaf Rapids, Manitoba, from a cabin along the Churchill River, I was struck by the realization of how intensely I wanted to take part, someday, in the Iditarod Trail Sled Dog Race. This race across Alaska, over 1,100 miles long, is the best-known and longest test of a long-distance dogteam. I knew all the reasons that I could *not* do it that coming season—no money, no sponsors, no experience in Alaska, a team perhaps not strong or trail-wise enough. These "reasons" were all familiar; I had lined them up and reviewed them mentally a thousand times.

But that day, with the weather cold and clear and my mood buoyed by the steady improvement of my young and eager dogteam, I wondered whether what was needed most of all was a simple leap of faith.

I could go on for years awaiting the perfect set of circumstances for my rookie run in the Iditarod—generous sponsors, a tough, experienced team, an entire season of Alaskan training and so on. But the likelihood of such a convergence of good luck and circumstance was,

I realized, about equal to the probability of being invited to dinner by Jessica Lange.

It was time, once again, to fly in the face of "good judgment," to quit thinking and start doing. I resolved that day to *enter* the 1986 Iditarod and to let that entry fee be the impetus that would eventually put my dogs and me at the starting line in Anchorage, come hell or high water. And Jessica never did stop by our cabin on the Churchill.

Two and a half months later, we were driving the Alaska Highway—Mitch Gilbert, Keizo Funatsu from Osaka, Japan, 14 sled dogs, Mitch's black lab, Mack and I. My $1,249 entry fee had been paid in full on the latest possible date, we had a fifth-place finish in the 1986 Beargrease behind us, a long list of sponsors and supporters had come forward to help us out, the truck was loaded, as always, to overflowing and we were bearing down on metropolitan Anchorage.

Our preparation for my rookie running of the Iditarod Trail would make an amusing, harrowing and at times ludicrous story in itself, but I fear that the account would stretch the limits of credulity. Suffice it to say that none of us would ever choose to go through it all again at the pace that the deadlines set for us.

There were long evenings of carving up beaver, salmon, horse and turkey meat for dog food, a tent and igloo training camp near the foothills of Denali, a mad spending spree in what we soon came to know as Los Anchorage and a particularly memorable evening in our concrete basement encampment when we arrived home to find the floor awash in six inches of water. In 43 seconds, Keizo ran through his entire repertoire of English-language profanity at least three times.

I don't think our Iditarod preparations were unusual. I have good reason to believe that every rookie Iditarod musher could tell a similar story of resolve and doubt, confusion and fumbling preparation. It's all part of the first run.

What follows is my story of the 1986 Iditarod Trail Sled Dog Race—the World Series of long-distance dog mushing. This account is not a guide to the trail, nor a detailed look at the techniques of Iditarod racing, nor an overview of the entire 1986 race. It is simply a *rookie's* story, a mixture of present-tense commentary and past-tense memory.

The Iditarod, although an event now known throughout the world and despite its 50 to 70 competitors and scores of associated people along the trail, is and always will be a solitary journey. Only some of it can be shared. The rest, the very essence of the race, can only be experienced.

March 1, Anchorage, Eagle River, Settler's Bay, Knik.

"7 a.m., Fourth Avenue, downtown Anchorage. It's just begun to get light here, a cold clear morning. Overnight, the pavement has been covered with snow that has been trucked in and packed down. As far up and down the avenue as I can see there are dog trucks and teams and people wearing headlamps are darting back and forth. A few spectators have arrived and they gather along the snow fence that cordons off the street.

"It's surprisingly quiet, considering that there are now 73 dogteams of 12 to 18 dogs apiece lining the street. I don't feel the tight knot of nerves in my gut that I expect will come a little later this morning. We still have three and one-half hours until we're out of the chute and on our way. Plenty of time to joke around with Mitch and Keizo, drink orange juice and fool with the dogs. . . ."

The hours passed quickly that Saturday morning. We had been awake at 4 a.m., to arrive downtown and take our place in the procession of dog trucks that would get everyone parked along Fourth Avenue in the proper position. The logistics of the Iditarod race are mind-boggling and those of its start are no exception. The start in downtown Anchorage is actually a false one. The teams run only 25 miles to Eagle River and are then trucked around the head of Cook Inlet to Knik, where they start again. For the first stretch, through the heart of Anchorage, a handler rides in the sled or is towed behind on a second sled, to assist the driver in case of any problems. Keizo rode with me that year.

"10:18. The sled's loaded for the run to Eagle River, the lines are laid out and the dogs are in harness. Two minutes and we'll start putting them in place. We're Number 48, with teams leaving at two-minute intervals. Okay—Morris and Beaver in lead, Jake and Henry at point, then Tex and Arnold, D. J. and Grayling, Magoo and Brew, Nipper and Yak and Eddie and Sister in wheel. A whole crew of people has appeared to help us up the street to the chute and we're moving. A few minutes ago, I was choked with emotion. Now it's time to race, time to get out of Anchorage and on the trail and I feel calm and happy. . . ."

That first day was frantic and nerve-wracking. The early morning scene downtown, the start, the 25-mile run to Eagle River, the drive to Settler's Bay, the restart, the short run to Knik checkpoint and then, finally, on out past the roads, past the crowds, into a thick spruce woods on a narrow winding trail. Toward nightfall, toward the Big Susitna River, toward the mountains, toward Nome.

We ran that evening for four hours out of Knik before stopping along the trail about 8 p.m. I melted snow for the dogs and made a broth of beaver meat and chicken for them to drink. They curled up and slept and I lay on the sled and tried to doze. It was windy and there were teams passing by on the trail every few minutes. At midnight we were on the move again, the dogs running well and the Rabbit Lake checkpoint about 35 miles ahead.

March 2, Rabbit Lake, Skwentna, Finger Lake.
"1:30 a.m., Day 2—we just hit Flathorn Lake and it's blowing hard across here. The trail is icy and wide and we just have to follow these markers on across. Some of them have been blown down or knocked over by other sleds and I can't quite tell for a half mile at a time whether we've still got the trail. Then there'll be a little orange marker shining ahead and I breathe easy for a while. This stretch has me nervous, since it's blowing so hard and the country is all unfamiliar. Napoleon is supposed to have said, 'There are no brave men at 3 a.m.' or something like that and right now I feel that cold, tired, worried state of mind coming on. There—we're into the alders now and climbing slightly off the lake. I see several headlamps behind me, off on wrong turns, sweeping back and forth in search of a marker. I set the hook behind a spruce and go up to undo a little tangle in the team. The dogs whine and bark impatiently. Dogs are great on nights like this—the worse things get, the more they love it!"

After leaving the Anchorage area, the trail crosses a 90-mile stretch of low spruce bog, gently rolling woods and several river valleys. It is country much like northern Minnesota. The trail conditions through this stretch were fair to poor, with the surface very hard-packed and filled with the washboard moguls of frequent snowmobile traffic.

We had been warned about one spot in particular—a nearly vertical drop of glare ice, down the 20-foot bank of the Big Susitna River. There I made an error that cost me several hours, by following another team up a side trail on the river—a route that had been marked similarly to the Iditarod Trail for a race earlier in the winter.

Finally, after a frustrating search through the wee hours of Sunday morning, we regained the race trail and banged and bounced our way to Rabbit Lake checkpoint, signing in there at 5:42 a.m.

I was heartened when the checker nodded toward a team and driver that were pulled off the trail just ahead and said, "That's Joe Runyan there." I was ready for a

121

break and the hours lost on the river had taken their toll on my team's enthusiasm. I decided to stay there and nap until 9:30.

"A little past noon, day two. We just signed into Skwentna. This is the first food-drop checkpoint on the race and really the first checkpoint of any significance. The river here is filled from bank to bank with dogteams, sleds, cookstoves, mushers, airplanes, snowmobiles, race officials and spectators. I've picked up my three sacks of food and supplies and carried them over to my sled, one at a time. Now I see why some drivers carry those little plastic sleds along in their loads. Dragging huge sacks of provisions around at these major stops is a real chore when you're tired. Right now I'll give the dogs a good feed of lamb and frozen mush. This is dry dog food soaked in liver broth and vitamins and frozen into blocks. Then I'll head up to the cabin for a bowl of stew for myself.

"Jim Ortman is here, flying a reporter from Anchorage along the race trail. He used to be a flight instructor of mine in Duluth and it's nice to see a familiar face. I figure we should pull out of here at 4 p.m. The first teams pulled out between 5 and 10 this morning. This is mile 148. From here it's 45 miles to Finger Lake."

The team ran very well between Skwentna and Finger Lake. We were climbing gradually into the Alaska Range on this stretch, the weather was clear and cold and as darkness fell their pace seemed to quicken. We arrived at Finger Lake at about 9:30 that evening. The snow there was over six-feet deep and with at least 20 teams at the checkpoint the food bags had to be hauled a long way.

I was feeling the aftermath of the hectic week prior to the race and the confusion of the first night out. After feeding the team, I slept for three hours and then prepared to head out. A loose wire in my headlamp suddenly broke completely and I was obliged to go back inside Gene Leonard's checkpoint cabin to fix it—a simple but frustrating process. The old 3 a.m. syndrome again. We finally headed out into the darkness at 4:20, bound for Rainy Pass.

March 3, Rainy Pass, Rohn Roadhouse.

"It's five in the morning and must be −25°. The waning moon is up and I've got Springsteen pounding through the earphones under my fur hat. The dogs are moving well and we're into the mountains now. I feel the exhilaration of the moment replace the sickening slow fatigue of a few hours ago. The moonlight, the dogs clipping along and the trail finally in good shape—I feel again like it's all worth it. Soon it will be light and Rainy Pass can't be more than 25 miles ahead. Just keep it together. . ."

But I didn't. Or at least I didn't as well as I could have, looking back with the humbling clarity of hindsight. Fatigue, though not a major factor yet, had begun to work on me. Just past the steep descent into the Happy River Gorge, itself a notorious piece of trail, we began the climb toward Rainy Pass.

Here, just after dawn, I again lost the trail and this time the blind alley led up and over the shoulder of a substantial ridge. I was following sled tracks, though, and did not realize my mistake until after we made a wild descent of a steep hill. Disgusted, I turned around and backtracked to where we had left the proper trail.

I had heard all about how rookies did such things all the time in this race, but somehow I'd figured I could keep the trail, first time and every time, for two weeks straight. Following this mix-up, I drove the dogs too hard into Rainy Pass Lodge.

Making up for lost time is a very difficult game to play in any race and that morning I succumbed to the temptation that I knew to be wrong. Tired, cold and out of food for both the dogs and myself, we pushed on toward the checkpoint and dipped into that reserve energy that shouldn't yet have been touched. That afternoon, I paid the price.

"11 a.m., Rainy Pass Lodge, cold and windy here and the team isn't getting very good rest. I'm concerned about their feet and am having a hell of a time getting salve and booties on them, with my bare hands freezing and the dogs not very amenable to my fiddling with them. Hope to get out of here by 2 this afternoon, but there's a lot to do between now and then. I should try for some sleep here, too, but it looks like that won't happen."

At 2:18 the team reluctantly trotted up the trail out of the Rainy Pass checkpoint. We were above treeline almost immediately and the wind had risen to a gale. The snow picked up by the wind made it difficult to follow the sled tracks from teams ahead of me. I was running behind a Norwegian musher, Rune Hesthammer, who was driving a team of excellent dogs leased from Susan Butcher. He was slowly pulling away from me.

Shortly after I lost sight of him I saw another team coming straight at us through the ground blizzard. As he came up, heading back into the checkpoint, I saw that it was Joe Redington. Joe, who is over 70 years old, is the founding father of the Iditarod race. Despite his age, he consistently places well and is known to have in his kennel some of the best long-distance dogs in the world.

As his team came by, he shouted at me through the ruff that was snugged up over most of his face: "My leader doesn't want to run into this wind." His team was high-tailing it for Rainy. I remember standing there surprised, wondering if maybe old Joe knew more about what lay ahead than I did.

That was about 3 p.m. We were in for a three-hour struggle up into that wind. At one point the dogs' eyes were so caked with blown snow that they could not keep the trail and when I stopped to wipe them clear everyone in the team was curled up in a ball within seconds. As I walked up and down the line, clearing snow from their eyes and shouting encouragement to them in what I hoped was a cheerful, convincing tone of voice, they gave me that universal look—the "You're out of your mind!" look.

We got back on the trail. Over the pass, the wind was strong enough at times to knock the dogs off their feet. As soon as we crested the pass, we dropped down into a little bowl on the shoulder of the mountain and there were three teams resting there—Bob Chlupach, Rune Hesthammer and John Barron. I pulled off the trail, gave the dogs a snack and rested them there for half an hour. Had I known what was ahead, I would not have given them more than a brief pause in that spot.

Dalzell Gorge, in that 1986 race, was the wildest stretch of trail I have ever sledded. We hit it just at dusk and before long it was dark. Sixteen miles of steep, icy trail twisting back and forth across the frozen bed of Dalzell Creek. Pieces of gear, bits of sled and scarred trees all attested to the passage of more than 20 teams ahead of me. There were places where the "trail" of glare ice tilted right toward a hole the size of a truck. Time after time, as my headlamp flashed ahead to the next stretch, I thought, "Well, we're goners now for sure."

And time after time, with absolutely no grace or semblance of finesse, we would squeak past the hole, the tree, the rock, the cliff, or whatever it was. If I had a nickel for every time my narrow 16-inch sled tipped over on that descent, I'd have earned enough money to buy ten wider ones!

After what seemed like hours, we flew out of the mouth of Dalzell Gorge and onto a broad mountain river. Here there was little snow and a new difficulty: overflow. This is water that lies atop river or lake ice and is kept unfrozen by the snow cover and current, even at brutally cold temperatures.

The trail markers had been scattered far and wide by the careening sleds of the front-runners and we picked our way down the river by trial and error. The trail cut over gravel bars, back onto the ice, up through the shoreline brush and through stretches where the water was well over one foot deep.

If my team had had any doubts as to my sanity on the ascent to Rainy Pass, that stretch down the river must have confirmed their worst hunch. We arrived at Rohn Roadhouse checkpoint at a full gallop—the gallop of a dogteam hell-bent on leaving behind the crazy fellow on the sled.

It was 9:37 p.m. Our crossing from Rainy Pass, 48 miles, had taken nearly seven and one half hours, during which the dogs had not rested for more than 50 minutes. I signed in and realized that the entire field of racers ahead of me was still at Rohn—no one had signed out yet and none were likely to do so until they had taken their 24-hour break. Each team in the race must spend at least 24 hours in one checkpoint somewhere along the route and this looked like the place where all the front-runners intended to satisfy that requirement. The word around the checkpoint was that the trail ahead had not yet been marked.

I was exhausted—more exhausted, I think, than at any other time on the entire race. My dogs were simultaneously keyed up and worn down. We would lay over for 24 hours. I found a place to pull into the woods, feed and look after the team, unroll my sleeping bag and pass out.

March 4, Rohn.

"It's morning, clear and cold. This is a beautiful spot, at the confluence of two rivers, surrounded by high peaks shining pink and blue in the sunlight. There must be over 30 teams parked here now and only one musher, rookie Mike Pemberton, has pulled out. Most of us are waiting out our 24-hour layovers.

"There is time—time to attend to details of gear and dog care, build a fire and grill a moose steak, talk with other mushers, think over the race and speculate on the stretch ahead.

"It is going to be a rough one. Reliable word is that there is no snow for over 50 miles of the next 90 and only marginal snow for the other 40. The trail has not been marked and without snow those who go behind will have no tracks to follow. I'm trying not to ponder too long on all of this.

"The team looks good today, though still tired. We're still near the front end of the race and anything can happen. Tonight at 10:30 we can leave here, just eight hours behind the very first team to have completed the layover. Everyone is here, names that until now I have only read about or seen briefly at the pre-race meetings—Rick Swenson, Lavon Barve, Joe Garnie, Susan Butcher, John Cooper, Dewey Halverson, Jerry Austin, Joe Runyan. Whoever will win this race is probably camped here somewhere. Although the atmosphere is friendly, there is an undercurrent of tension and anxiety. The race is well underway. None of the top drivers are awaiting some turning point down the trail to 'get serious.' And neither am I."

At Rohn, I jettisoned several items from my load and gave them to my pilot friend Jim Ortman. They included my camera, and while it only weighs a pound or so, my leaving of it reflected my state of mind at this stage of the race. I was not here to take pictures. There were photographers behind every bush. I was here to race and every moment that the camera might take from my efforts was a moment I could better spend tending to my dogteam, my gear, my food or my sleep. So away went the camera. As the race went on, I would regret that decision.

When my departure time drew near, I finished all the little chores that had filled my day. I packed the sled and lashed the load down, as if my life depended on it. Then I wandered down to the cabin that served as check-point headquarters to indulge myself in a little more of that precious, rare commodity for Iditarod mushers—time. To sit quietly in a warm cabin, filled with the chatter of a dozen other mushers and race officials, sip hot chocolate and just let one's weary mind wander, is a delight not easily described.

When my watch read 9:30 p.m. I pulled on my parka, strapped on my headlamp and walked out to hook up my team. I will never forget that lump-in-the-throat feeling of heading out from Rohn checkpoint in my first Iditarod. The cold, the darkness, with unknown trail ahead—those are moments of life lived on its keen edge. Those moments are reason enough to live such a life and run such a race.

The team had rested for 25 hours. As I harnessed them and swung the leaders out toward the trail, I knew it had been enough. The dogs were eager, lunging and whining and scrapping with their partners. My spirits soared—this would be a night to remember. This dog-team was ready and as tough, trailwise and crazy as they could be. At 10:29 p.m. the hook was pulled and we were down the trail like a shot, onto the gravel and bare ice of the river—flying, I thought, just flat-out flying.

March 5, The Farewell Burn.

"12:10 a.m. I just met Bill Cowart walking back along the trail. He is shaken and angry. His team is somewhere around here, with their noses filled by the scent of a moose. Bill is walking toward Rohn—he has given up on finding his team tonight—and he asked for a lift back toward the checkpoint when I offered to help him. But that is one thing I will not consider. This trail is like nothing I've ever been over, with 14 eager dogs in the middle of the night. It is nothing but a hard-packed, icy gouge through a tangle of stunted spruce and clumps of marsh grass. 'Bad' does not describe it. 'Suicidal' comes close. If I tried to carry Bill on my sled, there would soon be two of us walking back into Rohn without dogteams."

It was −10 or −20 degrees when I saw Bill Cowart walking back along the trail. I had never met him, but his name was familiar to me as the fellow who was running Herbie Nayokpuk's team that year. I shared a thermos of hot chocolate with him and tried to convince him to abandon his plan of walking back to Rohn. Most mushers' experiences with runaway teams have been that the dogs usually don't get very far before becoming either tangled or stopped by someone else. But Cowart, understandably upset, wasn't listening to any advice from a novice that night. As I moved on down the trail, still barely keeping control of my own team, the thought of him heading back toward Rohn troubled me. What would I do if I lost my team out here, I wondered. I felt vaguely guilty for passing him by and hoped that I might still get a chance to help him somehow.

The team and I crossed the Post River and climbed a steep icy chute on the far side. There, about a half mile past the river, was a team—neatly strung out and tied in the woods along the trail, all seemingly happy and healthy. I shouted a couple of times to see if anybody was around who might belong to those dogs. No answer.

It had to be Bill's team. He had asked me to signal him if I found his dogs. Out came my pistol, a .44 revolver that a friend had loaned me, in case of moose trouble on the trail. In the 1985 race, a moose had killed two of Susan Butcher's dogs when it became tangled up with her team.

I hauled the gun out of its holster, pointed it into the brush and squeezed the trigger. The memory of that explosion in the middle of the night still makes my ears ring. My team bolted, of course, and there I was with a loaded revolver in one hand, the handlebar of my sled in the other, careening down this god-awful trail trying to convince my lead dogs that I hadn't lost my marbles. Unbelievably stupid. I finally stopped the dogs, set the snowhook behind a substantial spruce tree and fired three rounds. By then, my dogs were in an absolute panic.

I looked at my watch. 12:45 a.m. I figured I had come at least three miles since I'd seen Bill and during that time he'd been walking at a good clip in the opposite direction. Plus, he had a hat and a hood on over his ears. He probably couldn't hear the shots.

All I could do would be to turn around, go back and find him and tell him his team was ahead. Or I could just go on, keep my own dogs rolling and make some miles before taking a rest break about 2:30 a.m. It was not an easy decision. Perhaps, in hindsight, I decided wrong. I turned back.

I nearly smashed up my sled on the trip back, descending that icy chute onto the Post River. By the time I got to Bill, I'd met at least four teams head on and we had struggled to maneuver our dogs past each other on the narrow trail. With each delay I knew that Cowart was getting further and further ahead of me. I was past the limits of patience by the time I caught him. I told him where his team was, being less than friendly about it, and it was 3:45 a.m. when I again passed his dogs tied there in the woods. It was time to rest my own team. The night was shot, our momentum dissipated.

"It's mid-afternoon at the Farewell Lakes. Still clear and cold. Douglas Sheldon and Fred Jackson, both Eskimos from Kotzebue, just took off down the trail after a break here. We shared coffee, some muktuk, whale blubber and some ugruk, bearded seal meat.

"My spirits are up again, after the long confused night. Saw Bill Cowart earlier today and he's ahead of us again with that fast team of Herbie's moose hounds. Just had some welcome news—the whole lead pack of mushers is only 30 miles ahead, at most, still picking their way through the completely snowless country. This report came from a Super Cub pilot and a photographer who landed on this lake a few minutes ago. At 4 p.m. my dogs will have had a good snooze and we'll take off. We're behind my projected schedule by a ways, but we still could make Nikolai sometime tonight. We're already 16 hours out of Rohn."

Luckily, I did not know that afternoon just how crazy the coming night would get. This was the start of the Farewell Burn—40 miles or so of burned-over scrub spruce and tundra grass, almost completely flat and featureless. The trail-marking crew had written this section off after trying to run snow machines through it and ending up with a couple of broken ribs. The leaders had been led through here by Roger Nordlum in his Super Cub, flying low and pointing the way to the far side of the burn.

By nightfall, I was about two thirds of the way across the burn. My headlamp was on the blink again, literally, and the trail was becoming almost impossible to keep. There were widely scattered patches of old crusty snow and some runner tracks showed on them. The trouble was, almost every patch of snow had some tracks on it and no two sets led in the same direction. Considering the time I had been delayed the night before, there were probably more than 40 teams ahead of me by then— including more than a few lost, bewildered rookies like myself.

The dogs were amazing through that stretch. Mile after mile, the sled lurched and bumped along over grass and rock, forcing them to abandon all semblance of a cruising trot, lower their heads and *haul.* Still, they kept the speed fairly high and by far the weakest member of our team was—guess who? I was exasperated. My emotions had swung from low to high and back again so many times, so abruptly, that I had begun to doubt whether they would ever level off.

Then, just at twilight, we lurched out of the frying pan and into the fire—a scrub and tundra fire, burning uncontrolled across the horizon ahead of us. It had evidently been started by a careless signal flare, when the trail-marking crew signaled an aircraft.

It was March 5, in the heart of Alaska, at −20 degrees and my dogteam was running straight toward a wildfire. *That's* how little snow there was on the 1986 Iditarod Trail!

As it got fully dark, I could see headlamps flashing ahead of me and behind me. Several teams seemed to be moving off to the north of the fire. At this time I still thought that perhaps the flames were actually numerous campfires of lost teams strung out ahead of us. I began chasing a single light ahead of me and caught up to another musher who was resting his team.

"Hi, what's your name?"

"Dave Olesen."

"Martin Buser, Dave. Hell of a deal we're getting into here, eh?"

"I'll say. What's with all the fires?"

"It's a forest fire, just burning on its own. I heard the leaders started it. My dogs are getting sick of this; what do you say we trade off for a while?"

"Sounds good. I'll go out front for a bit. We're bearing just north of the fire then?"

"Yeah, or even right straight toward it for now."

Off we went. We must have spent at least an hour zigzagging through the scrub spruce and grass, here finding a trail, here losing it, our lead dogs getting fed up with us and Martin and I getting fed up with them, each other, the race and the world at large. It was about 9:30 that night and Martin was out front when he halted his team and I came up behind him.

"Mine need a break."

"Yeah, mine too. You got the trail?"

"Ha! I don't know, Dave. I don't know."

Soon we had fed our dogs what little we each had left to offer. We were hunkered down beside Martin's sled, lighting a cookstove and trying to scrape together enough snow for a pot of tea. The wind was blowing hard from the northeast and pushing the bright glow of the wildfire away from us. We laughed and cursed and talked, then dozed.

March 6, Nikolai, McGarth.

At 2:30 a.m., Martin hooked up his team and pulled out, to make another attempt at finding the trail into

Nikolai. I remained where I was, sleepy and discouraged, until dawn and then hit the "trail."

My team, well-rested, if a little hungry and thirsty, clipped right along. We quickly found some old trail markers and crossed the remainder of the burn, passed the old Salmon River roadhouse and signed into Nikolai at 12:12 p.m., March 6th. We had been almost 38 hours on the 97 miles from Rohn. The leaders had left Nikolai the evening before. The run through The Burn had been some buggy ride.

"Mid-afternoon in Nikolai. Word is that the trail ahead is good. I feel optimistic. The dogs look good. We're on a new stretch of the trail. Nikolai is a native town and it's nice to have reached the inhabited part of the Interior. Dan MacEachen is here, taking his 24 hours and working on his busted-up sled. I guess I was lucky to get through the Burn with my sled more or less intact. And myself as well. Bill Cowart is here and he's in rough shape. He has a puncture wound in one cheek, a big bump on the head and the remains of a slight concussion. He hasn't scratched, but it's got to look like an awfully long haul to Nome from here.

"I'm going to leave here about five and run more or less straight to McGrath. It's going to get cold tonight, probably close to −50°. I'm so glad to be through that last stretch that Nome seems just around the corner! Less than 800 miles to go . . . the Kuskokwim, the Yukon and the coast. I still have all the dogs I started with. Though their feet are a little worse for wear, they seem to be getting into the groove. Coming in here this morning they looked good."

The events between Rohn and Nikolai changed the race for me. I suspect that this could be said for many mushers, especially the rookies. The Burn in 1986 was, by the accounts of those who are long familiar with that infamous stretch, the worst it had ever been in 14 years of Iditarod racing. We arrived in Nikolai a changed team, the dogs and I. The leaders were well ahead of us, as were many teams with whom I felt we should be running. It was time to begin a steady, cautious game of catch-up. Time also to remind myself that the first and foremost goal was to get the team to Nome. And to do that, I knew, depended upon keeping them as happy, interested and physically fit as I possibly could.

Arriving in Nikolai, the race's first village checkpoint, marked another turning point. From here on, the checkpoints were mostly small settlements—places where the residents of the country lived and worked. This was a welcome change, a new aspect of the race that I had long anticipated. My sleeping bags were hung to dry in a schoolteacher's home. I stopped by the café for a cup of coffee before heading out. In the long, wearying miles of solitary travel, these little nuances of village life were a boost. I was amazed by the enthusiasm shown by the local people, even for us "middle of the pack" mushers.

My dogs rested all afternoon in the sunshine and at 5:36 p.m. we pulled out for McGrath. I remember that as a good stretch of trail. The dogs moved along well, ate and drank well at our midway break and they came into the village of McGrath on the bounce, just before midnight.

The night was clear and the northern lights shimmered over the lights from the town as we came down the Kuskokwim River. I signed in and was directed to a nearby home for a rest. Another musher was just leaving there and the entire family that lived there was sound asleep. I quietly did my chores and fell asleep in my trail clothes on their living room floor.

March 7, McGrath, Takotna, Ophir.
"Beebeep-beebeep-beebeep . . . the alarm, where is it . . . beep-beebeep . . . oh for criminy sakes . . . there! Oh yeah, the floor, McGrath, 4:30 a.m., dog food, water, booties, get up, get going, damn, I'm tired . . . somebody coming in, John Wood."

The fog of waking from a too-brief sleep, again and again, was becoming all too familiar. This was only McGrath, not even halfway. I stumbled outside, the dogs were curled up in the cold night; the air on my skin helped wash away that dizzy, nauseous feeling of awakening. I gathered up the food I had thawed for the team and roused them as I went down the line with it. Then the familiar ritual of packing the sled, piling my unused supplies in the yard of the house (for use by my hosts' dogteam), getting my layers and layers of clothing sorted out and hooking up the 14 harness toggles. Back on the street, Beaver and Morris in lead, we made our way through town to the checkpoint and out along the trail. It was 6:30 a.m. Maybe next year I'd see McGrath in the light of day.

"Cold—I bet it's −50° or lower up in here. We're threading our way up and over some foothills, away from the Kuskokwim, toward Takotna. It's light now and beautiful with the pink of sunrise on some distant ranges south and west. Endless mountain and river country in every direction—I bet I can see over 100 miles to every horizon. Haven't seen another team on this stretch."

Takotna is a small mining town with a checkpoint at the community hall. There was warm water there to thaw broth for the dogs and breakfast waiting inside for passing mushers. I was there an hour and 15 minutes, before starting the long climb out of town on a narrow road.

Ophir is 450 miles into the race. It was March 7, a Friday afternoon, when we pulled in there. A week on the trail, night and day, had altered my awareness, my consciousness—I was a different person. Life was the race, day to day and hour to hour. Fatigue was the normal state of existence. The dogs were my partners, the trail was our reason for living. Iditarod had become a state of being. It would remain so for another nine days and 700 miles. The vivid stream of my memories blurs into a montage of sights, sounds and events, all accompanied by that strange blend of tension and exhaustion. . . .

"Mid-afternoon, Ophir. Can't find the sheath for the axe. I stumble around and around my little spot along the trail, muttering, kicking the snow, sorting through the sled load. Finally, I go inside the small house that serves as the checkpoint headquarters, eat a bowl of stew and fall asleep in a corner . . . At 6:24 p.m., groggy and disgruntled about nothing in particular, I call to my lead dogs and we move down the trail, along the Innoko River, toward Cripple."

Mileage estimates along the Iditarod Trail vary from accurate to absurd. Before the race, we were all given a sheet of figures listing checkpoints, prominent landmarks and the mileages between each point. This, along with a map that I purchased (most racers don't carry one since the trail is plainly marked), had been my guide for planning along the way. But there were differences of opinion, it seemed, at every checkpoint. At Ophir, I was told it was "an easy 50" to Cripple, despite the paper in my sled bag that put the mileage at 70.

March 8, Cripple Landing.
"6 a.m., pitch dark, cold and where the hell is Cripple? We've been on the trail nearly 12 hours and I've thought that the team has been running well. We've taken several stops, but nothing over 90 minutes. Cold tonight and the trail has been excellent. If we don't make Cripple within the hour, we'll have to stop short for a substantial rest. Are we lost? There! Off to the left, through the trees, headlamps and firelight. The smell of woodsmoke. 'All right, let's giddup, take it on in . . . good dogs!' 50 miles, my ass!"

Cripple Landing checkpoint was the official halfway point of the 1986 Iditarod. Here at about 1 a.m. on March

7, Jerry Austin collected the $2,000 in silver coins put up by Alascom, Inc. for the first musher halfway to Nome. Cripple was a tent camp and a well-organized checkpoint. It was there that I was perked up by the sight of several mushers whom I had not seen since leaving Rohn—Joe Redington, Nina Hotvedt, Peter Sapin, Ted English. These were the teams I wanted to be running and racing with. So maybe we *could* make up for the Burn.

Peter, who is from Grand Marais in Minnesota, seemed down as we talked together. He had ten dogs and was not too happy with the way they looked. But he seemed to have been doing all right and maybe was just wrestling with the Iditarod blues. As the sun came up at Cripple, he started down the trail and I wished him luck. I enjoyed a good breakfast around the campfire, my dogs were sleeping and had eaten well and I felt good. As Nina, a young Norwegian rookie, hooked up her team and pulled out, I yelled to her that I was going to catch her in Unalakleet and race her to Nome from there.

"Old Joe is hurting. Over 70 years old, a wiry man with a quick smile and a soft voice, he tosses meat to his dogs and mutters to them as he packs his sled. The Burn has taken it out of him—his gait is stiff and his face is drawn. I can sense his disappointment at his position in the race, here at the half-way mark. But he smiles to me and asks how it's going. 'Better by the mile,' I answer and this morning I believe it. He smiles again and turns his leaders out onto the trail. I head for a tent marked 'QUIET—MUSHERS ASLEEP' and set my alarm clock for 2:30 p.m."

From Cripple to Ruby is the longest stretch between food drops—132 miles, according to the official sheet. Looking ahead to this stretch, I tried to feed my team as much as they'd eat in Cripple. Still, the sled was filled to the brim with supplies when we hit the trail. I left my pistol with one of the checkers at Cripple, for safe return to Anchorage. From Cripple on, the threat of moose along the trail was said to be negligible.

About 5 p.m. we started out, through rolling spruce hills dotted with small lakes and drained by tiny streams. The snow was deep, but the trail was packed hard. The dogs seemed slow in the late afternoon hours, perhaps from overeating. At 7:30 p.m. we stopped and I set my alarm for 9 p.m. At 10:30 p.m. I woke with a start, fumbled with my headlamp, pulled the dogs to their feet and headed on. It was bitterly cold again; in the darkness the team scampered along.

March 9, Sulatna Crossing, Ruby.

We arrived at Sulatna at 4 a.m. to find a wall tent marked by a single kerosene lamp. Asleep were two other mushers and a couple of the checkpoint staff. Once my team was fed and bedded down, I went into the tent and had a cup of soup with the checker. He was from Anchorage and this was his first Iditarod, too.

We had an interesting discussion about the "athletic" nature of the race. One pet peeve of mine is the tendency of many people to regard dog mushers as the athletes in a sled dog race, when it is the dogs themselves who are the athletic competitors. The fellow in the tent at Sulatna Crossing, at 5 a.m., was bending my ear about how he figured dog drivers must be the most tough, physically fit athletes in the world. I didn't agree and we went around and around trying to define athlete, competitor and toughness, until finally at a brief pause in the debate I fell fast asleep right where I sat. I woke briefly, shuffled over to the corner of the tent, asked the fellow to wake me at 7 a.m. and passed out. My dogs had run 555 miles in the last eight days and I was getting pretty tired myself!

"8:30 a.m. and we're just out of Sulatna. The trail here is actually some sort of road. Not a highway, certainly, but in summer probably an access route for 4-wheel-drive vehicles and Cats. This is gold mining country and the rolling hills are

littered with the evidence of that—blazes, side roads, old machinery and scrap metal rusted beyond recognition. Morris is running back in the middle of the team today and Beaver and Tex are out front setting a pretty good pace. I still have every one of the dogs I started with and I've begun to fantasize about getting all of them to Nome.

"Just got caught and passed by Douglas Sheldon, but he had his whip out and was cracking that as he pulled away. I don't think he'll last long if that's how they're running. In this race, or any other long race for that matter, you keep your dogs happy—not scared. I've begun singing and chattering to mine fairly constantly now and they seem to like that. Still have some foot problems in the team, some worsening, others improving. We'll get there. My friend Catie Maloney and her fiancé are ahead in Ruby, so today I've got a little extra incentive—there's a familiar face up the trail. Also, the faces of those traveling at about my pace have begun to be the faces of friends and companions instead of strangers."

Ahead, too, was the Yukon River and the prospect of reaching that made Nome suddenly seem much closer. By this time, I had begun to appreciate the wisdom behind the seemingly simple advice that rookies hear so often before the race—"Just remember, it's a long way to Nome." As we headed over the hills along the Yukon Valley and then caught a glimpse of the broad river itself, the sheer magnitude of Alaska brought a lump to my throat and a mist to my eyes. No one can ever *tell* anyone else how far it is from Anchorage to Nome. Numbers are without meaning and words fail.

"Ruby is a village perched on a steep bank of the Yukon and here I've been escorted up a side trail to the home of a couple who are friends of Catie and Tom. The dogs seem happy here; perhaps they remember Catie from her time with them at Outward Bound in Minnesota. She raised and trained a couple of these guys as pups. It's good to see a friend. She tells me of the racers ahead, how they and their teams looked, what the word

on the trail ahead has been, how long most teams have rested in Ruby. It's dark again now and I must sleep awhile. I will leave at 2 a.m., down the river toward Galena. 58 miles."

March 10, Galena.

Cold. When I woke to leave Ruby and dashed outside to grab something from the sled, I remember saying, "Geez, it feels pretty warm out." But by the time we were on the river and moving down the ice, it was obvious that this was to be the coldest stretch of trail so far. I learned later that the temperature dropped below −50 degrees that night along much of the central Yukon River valley.

There weren't many times on the 1986 Iditarod when the day-to-day weather was much of a factor, but cold of that depth soon takes a toll on dogs and drivers. The darkness along the river that night seemed somehow deepened by the cold. At one point, I stopped to rest and Frank Torres of McGrath came up alongside. We rested together—by that I mean the *dogs* rested while we chopped food for them and drank warm fruit juice around Frank's charcoal stove.

Kari Skogen from Norway pulled up and she had just seen wolves along the trail. In the darkness, she had watched six animals trot down the riverbank in single file, just ahead of her team. Thinking it must be a dog-team, she had strained to make out the sled. With only six dogs, it wouldn't be an Iditarod team, but perhaps a trapline team—at 4 a.m. at −50?

There was no sled. The single-file formation dissolved and the tall dark shapes trotted out toward the river's wide expanse, then turned to parallel Kari's team. After "too long a time" they disappeared again into the darkness.

"There are good checkpoints and lousy checkpoints. I think it depends almost completely on my mood and on this race that goes from one extreme to the other. It's mid-afternoon

at Galena, the sun is too bright, the dogs are restless and at the same time exhausted and I feel about as cordial as a Mafia hit man. I plan to leave here this evening and travel in tandem with Kari Skogen. She suggested this—maybe she's still thinking about those wolves. Anyway, our teams might appreciate the chance to run consistently with some other dogs. This is done quite often from this point in the race onward, even by some of the hotshots. I'm happy to give it a try. Right now, though, I'm just wallowing in my own crankiness. Time to take a nap."

March 11, Nulato, Kaltag.

"Out on the Yukon, 2:20 a.m. Left Galena at 7:30 and now that seems like days ago. Here on the river the trail has been like a mirage, or a wild hallucination. The circle of light from my headlamp throws strange shapes into view—slanting pressure ridges, sand spits, off to each side somewhere the thin line of spruces outlined against stars. I doze, wake, turn to see a headlamp behind me.

"We blunder up near the village of Koyokuk, not a checkpoint, not even on the race trail. A couple of village dogs bark, I pull out the map, realize where we are, head off downriver, trying to figure out, literally, which way is up. Now there is some ice fog in the air and above it some high rock riverbank. Another team comes into sight, resting beside the trail. . . . 'On by, on by, good dogs. . .' Still they run and run and run. They, at least, have not lost their minds out here on this dark cold river."

At 5:30 a.m. we signed into Nulato. Actually it was Old Nulato, since the new village is either up or down the river a short distance. I never understood which. There were several old log buildings in use, a warm wood stove and good resting places for the dogs. No one was around except a couple of checkpoint helpers and a ham radio operator.

The hams form a vital link in the race organization. They are at each checkpoint, relaying information or "dog traffic" as they call it on the air: "CSM, KZY has some dog traffic for you—Number 48 into Nulato at 0530, with 14, out at 1015 with 14. Number 27 into Nulato. . ." and on and on, day after day. They seemed to enjoy this work, being a part of the race, being the ones "in the know."

At Nulato I rested the team again and talked about the Beargrease Race with Steve Bush from Aniak. My fifth-place finish in January 1986 was noticed by a few mushers in Alaska and in some ways it haunted me during my first Iditarod. But the Iditarod is a far cry from the Beargrease and from Nulato at 6 a.m. on March 11, the "John Beargrease Sled Dog Marathon" resembled a Cub Scout picnic in my imagination. I told that to Steve and we both laughed.

"Just past noon, between Nulato and Kaltag. The day is warm and the dogs are losing their momentum. I'm pushing on toward Kaltag more out of stubbornness than good sense. The factor of cold has been replaced by the factor of warmth and the afternoon is going to be a real slog, I'm afraid. It's not 'warm' by any standards other than those of an Alaskan winter, but the dogs are showing the effects of the sunshine, combined with what I think is just plain boredom with this flat river trail. Onward."

We arrived in Kaltag at 3:30. Then, more than ever, the talk in the checkpoints was of the race's front-runners along the trail ahead, closing in on Nome. It was Garnie and Butcher and it was a close race. News like this always gave me a boost, rather than being discouraging. Nome *was* ahead—these people whose names filled the first page of the sign-in sheet at Kaltag were almost there and there was my name, 27th or so and still with all my dogs. We were doing all right. At Kaltag, the veterinarian told me that he had seen "many" teams come through looking "a lot more ragged" than my own. This was a lift and

I made up my mind to keep thinking like a dog musher and not just fumble my way to the finish line.

It was obvious from the sign-in sheet that most teams had taken a good long rest in Kaltag. Ahead lay 90 miles up and over the Kaltag Mountains on the "portage" to the coast of Norton Sound and the Bering Sea. At 11 p.m. I walked out to check the dogs. My feeling then, from their response to my cheerful mumbling, was that I would be wise to give them three more hours. Feeling confident in that decision, I lay down again.

March 12, Unalakleet.

At 2:30 a.m. on the twelfth morning of the race, I slipped the last harness toggle into place on a tugline and turned toward the sled. Morris was back in lead, along with Beaver. We had been in Kaltag nearly 11 hours. I had just seen Dan MacEachen for the first time since Nikolai and it had been good to talk briefly with him. We had talked before the race of running together for a while, but by Kaltag I was wondering if that would happen. His team of sharp Redington dogs had been plagued by sickness up to that point, but they were coming on strong. I figured he would pass me on the coast.

The dogs were eager when we left Kaltag. As I swung onto the runners, they pulled the hook and bolted down the trail. They hadn't done that in days! As we climbed away from Kaltag, they were like a new team, fresh and eager and our Yukon River doldrums fell behind. Dawn came, pink and golden, to the crests of the Kaltag Range. Soon we were at timberline, crossing the divide into the drainage of the Unalakleet River. The dogs flushed a ptarmigan from alongside the trail and it hurtled straight into my chest as we drove by. I laughed aloud at my sudden panic. The dogs broke into a lope as I laughed and for a mile or two we just flew along the trail. It was wonderful to see them feeling so good, with the final 300 miles ahead.

"Mid-afternoon, on the broad tundra plain sloping down toward the coast. Now it is warm and not just by comparison to the nights on the Yukon. I imagine it is at least 25°. I just stopped to pull off my clothes and changed to flannel-lined blue jeans, a cotton anorak with a wolverine ruff, sunglasses and a baseball cap. Stowed away are the layers of clothes I've had on for over a week and what a refreshing change! Not so refreshing, though, is the view ahead. The tundra is brown and brings back plenty of recent memories from our struggle across the Farewell Burn. Hardly enough snow here to tell where the trail is, but it's been marked well so far by spruce pole tripods. The dogs have lost their zip again in this warmth and I'm hemming and hawing with myself over the choice of waiting for darkness or continuing on to Unalakleet. We'll see how this goes for a few more miles."

With the 20/20 vision of hindsight, I see that push to Unalakleet as one of my biggest mistakes in the later part of the race. Had we rested and continued on at dark, we would have been able to stay a short while in the village and then could have moved on toward Shaktoolik, still in the dark. As it turned out, we pulled in just at dusk, tired, and had to run around town trying to find the place where I could tend the dogs and let them rest. It was the first and only checkpoint on the race where I felt somewhat abandoned by the race organization. This was the night of *the* finish in Nome and everyone's interest was, understandably, focused on that.

March 13, Unalakleet, Shaktoolik.
"Midnight, in a family's living room in Unalakleet. Susan has just won the race. I sit and watch the television reports and joke a little with my hosts about how I'd better make my move pretty soon or I'll never catch her. I'm setting my alarm for 3 a.m. and will leave then. I need to drop my three youngest dogs here—D. J., Brew and Nipper—all two-year-olds in their first racing season. They've come far enough and while they're

still capable of going on, I think the team will do better without them. Coming clear to the coast at their age isn't easy and they all seem to have had enough."

For a while, I wondered if we would *ever* get out of Unalakleet. I slept right through my trusty alarm clock and rolled over at 6:30 a.m., three and one half hours behind my planned schedule. What followed was a long couple of hours of fumbling with gear and making arrangements for the dropped dogs. At 9:30 a.m. we at last made our way out of the snowless village, winding along on gravel paths beyond the city dump and up into the brown hills north along the coast.

"We can't say we weren't warned. But still, after all those nice white miles in the Interior, it is a rude shock to once again find the Iditarod Trail full of rock and ice and sand and grass— with every so often a fleck of old, dirty snow. Now it's on to Shaktoolik and mile by mile I'm getting another rude surprise. For years I've pictured this last coastal stretch of the race to be much like the sea ice journey I made on Hudson Bay in 1980— flat, white, with a pressure ridge here and there and fast. Wrongo, moose face. Here we have it—steep grades up and down, the trail a 12-inch ribbon of old snow on brown hillsides, the pack-ice miles away. Up these hills, a musher can outrun his sled. And down the hills—it might not be too hard to do the same. Arrgh . . . it's hard to keep these dogs happy when I feel like screaming and kicking something!"

A few miles later I came upon Steve Bush. We stopped our dogs together and found that we were in equally exasperated states of mind. We tried to joke and commiserate as the dogs lay sprawled on the withered grass in the warm sun.

"Where'd you get most of your team from?"

"These dogs? I picked these out down at the morgue. . ." And so on. Black humor.

Steve and I traveled together the rest of the way to Shaktoolik. The final 17 miles were along a narrow slough and here the northeast wind built to gale force. On the glare ice of the slough, it was possible only to take either a crosswind or downwind heading. For some reason I still don't understand, whenever the dogs would try to trot at an angle upwind or down, they would lose their footing on the smooth ice and fall down in a tangle of paws, legs, tails and tuglines. Finally, the buildings of Shaktoolik came into sight and we made our way to the school that was checkpoint headquarters. By this time, about 5:30 p.m., the windstorm was in full swing and it was clearly going to have to ease off a bit before this rookie left Shaktoolik.

"I'm going to drop Sister here. The only female in the team, she's been working like a trooper most of the way, but her pads are in rough shape and I think she'll just become a burden on the crossing to Koyuk. A young Eskimo boy named Leo is taking her over to his house tonight and will get her on the plane tomorrow. I pat her a couple of times and the two of them walk off into the windblown village. About five teams, including us, plan to leave here at first light in the morning."

March 14, Shaktoolik, Koyuk.

At 8 a.m. on the 14th, my leader Morris led us out of Shaktoolik, head-on into the wind. It certainly was nothing close to the gale that had blasted the 1985 race, but it was a good, stiff coastal blow. I was proud of old Morris as he put his head down and led the parade out of town—Steve Bush, John Wood, Kari Skogen, Martin Buser, Dan MacEachen, Gordon Brinker and one more team I can't recall. We did not keep the lead for long and a few of the teams passed us and flew almost instantly out of sight. We were slowing down. After we had crossed 14 miles of rolling tundra, the trail dropped down to the ice of Norton Sound. From there, stretching away as far as I could see, was a line of spruce pole tripods set into the sea ice—the trail to Koyuk, 35 miles ahead.

"It's good to be out on the ice. The wind has begun to drop and again I wish it were not so warm this afternoon. The

pink roof of a large building at Koyuk is shimmering on the horizon and at times it feels as though it is actually moving away from us despite our steady progress. The dogs seem to have a peculiar gait on this glare ice. I call it the 'glare ice shuffle.' It is a trot, but with more vertical motion than forward progress and it is slow! It reminds me of a person trying to run on a wet skating rink, without sliding. We should make Koyuk by 4:30 or so. It's been a good day—good to get out of those snowless brown hills and out on the open sea ice."

Koyuk was a good checkpoint and I got a chance there to talk and joke with some of the other mushers. At this point, Nome seemed just around the corner and we were all feeling a little punchy. The race had been won and it looked like we'd all make it to the finish line in good form.

My troubles started when I tried to leave. I signed out at 11:05 p.m., with a glance at the topo map showing the next stretch of trail to Elim. It was sea ice at first, then inland over some hills, then back on the ice, for a total of either 48 or 62 miles, depending on which estimate one chose to believe. With help from an Eskimo, I headed out on the ice and began to follow the markers leading away from town.

Twenty minutes out, the team was running well and there seemed to be a headlamp several miles ahead of us. Then I began to doubt whether I was on the right trail and soon I had convinced myself that we were backtracking on the trail from Shaktoolik. With a barrage of cursing, I turned the team around and they ran back to Koyuk. We arrived at midnight, only to be assured by a contingent of local experts that I had indeed been on the trail to Elim. As I swung the dogs around again, fuming with myself, the leaders balked. I couldn't blame them. I couldn't bed them down in Koyuk to while the cool night hours away either. After a few sharp words to Morris and Tex, I was moving down the ice again, a little wiser and an hour later, with a nearly mutinous dogteam.

March 15, Elim, Golovin, White Mountain.

"On the Iditarod, time changes. The numbers on a clock or a watch become merely that—numbers, without the attached feeling of a day's start, middle and end. Is it 3 a.m. or 3 p.m.? Who knows? Who cares? Just run and rest, run and rest, feed them and water them and check their feet, change sled runners, tie down the load and take a nap and on and on as the miles fall away behind us. Evening comes and twilight brings the instinct to stop, make camp, build a fire, ward off the darkness and the cold. But this is the race, the Iditarod Trail. At dusk we check our headlamps, flick on the lights, follow the markers, keep moving.

"It's a state of mind and after a while a state of being. Crazy? Certainly! But also somehow appealing and worthwhile in the lessons that come from it, in the state of mind I'm talking about.

"Like tonight—it's the trail to Elim, along the shacks of Moses Point. We're out on the edge of the continent in the middle of a winter night and there is nothing else. Just these dogs and this trail, snow and ice and darkness. It's spooky, if you let it catch you in a certain frame of mind, especially when you're exhausted and disappointed and not sure exactly where you are. The dogs keep going—I don't know how. I envy them, their unthinking, unflinching perseverance at moments like this. Envy them and depend on them, as much as they depend on me."

That trail to Elim, only one night short of Nome, was a long one for many teams. There was a mist in the air. There were many false trails, wrong turns and short-cuts to mislead tired minds. We made it through there without too much trouble, but it was the most delirious, hallucinogenic night of the race for me. As it grew light, we passed an old F.A.A. station and then followed a beautiful shoreline of granite topped by spruce. Rounding a headland, we climbed a short hill up from the sea ice and signed into the picturesque village of Elim.

There I was greeted by Fritz Saccheus, who shook my hand and said, "Welcome to Elim, Dave! I've been waiting for you!"

"Sorry to keep you," I answered. "I'd planned to get here a couple of days ago!" and he laughed. Then we went down the lane to his house, where I began the familiar routine of feeding and watering my tired dogs. They seemed to be doing pretty well, but the long night had taken its toll on us all. I remember Elim through a kind of haze, as a person remembers the events that went on around them while they were somehow incapacitated.

I stayed in Elim just long enough to tend to the dogs and have a stack of pancakes. There I dropped Arnold from my team—a veteran of many races but one of the most inconsistent dogs I've had. After a word of thanks to Fritz and Bessie, I got the team up and moving, out over rough pack ice down the coast to the southwest. It was 30 miles to Golovin and 23 from there to White Mountain. That was the last food drop and all teams were required to remain there for at least four hours. It was 9:30 a.m. when we arrived in Elim and just past noon when we left. I knew then what another Iditarod musher had meant when he said of an especially hospitable checkpoint: "I wanted to spend the rest of my life there!"

"This is powerful, eerie country, it seems to me. We just crested a divide on the peninsula that separates Elim from Golovin, forming Cape Darby. As we came over the top, there was a roaring wind behind us, a warm moist wind carrying sleet and freezing drizzle. Again the land is almost devoid of snow and the pulling is hard for the dogs. We are stopped alongside a shelter cabin and for the first time since we left Anchorage the team is refusing everything I offer them—beaver, lamb, salmon, even cream cheese. They just want to sleep and so for a few moments we sleep together, me lying down on the gravel of the trail between my leaders, Beaver and Morris, an arm around each of them. . . . I talk softly to them and pet them and am filled with amazement at all they've done in these

*last two weeks. . . . Taking a little piece of beaver meat, I start
to give them a bite at a time and soon they're all eating again. . .*

*"There are ten of us now, my dogs and me. Jerry Raychel
comes down over that windy crest, into the strange calm on this
side. I watch him come on for a long time and when he reaches
me his team goes by and my dogs follow. . . . We move out onto
the smooth bare ice of Golovin Bay and my dogs go into that
glare-ice shuffle of theirs. . . . The wind is to our side now, as
we head straight north up the bay to the Golovin checkpoint. . . .
Just a short stop there and it's on across the Golovin Lagoon,
just at dark, bound for White Mountain. . . . I feel like we
could be moving in a dream and wonder if perhaps I am still
asleep back in Koyuk or Unalakleet. . . . How can I tell for
sure?"*

At 10:10 p.m. I signed into White Mountain. My
team had faded badly on the river coming in and I was
concerned for them. It seemed to me that there was nothing greatly wrong with any of them, but that they had
finally lost the *trust* that is so vital on this race and on
any long journey by dogteam. Veterans of the Iditarod
have always been certain that a dog knows when it gets
close to Nome, *if* it has been there before and will carry
on through those last grueling stretches of trail. Even if
a few dogs in the team have the confidence that comes
from a past run along the coast, the rookie dogs can sense
the assurance of the veterans and persevere.

Not a single one of my team had ever run that trail
before. By the 15th day their trust in my wisdom and
integrity was rapidly waning. As far as they knew, this
might go on forever and lately the rests had been ridic-
ulously brief. They were sleepy and it was impossible to
convey to them the fact that in less than 24 hours this
long race, this long season, would be finished.

March 16, White Mountain, Safety, Nome.

White Mountain was another of the several checkpoints that I never saw in daylight. By Iditarod race rules,
each team must spend at least four full hours there before

beginning the final push to Nome. There is a thorough check of the team by a veterinarian and mushers drop any dogs that might have trouble making the final 70-some miles to Nome. Tex was the only dog to leave my team at White Mountain. He had been a gem for me for the entire race, but a cut in one of his pads had become painfully inflamed over the past 24 hours. It was disappointing to leave him behind with so short a distance remaining, but it would have been cruel to have kept him in the team.

(A 1988 rule change has given teams the option of taking their mandatory rest at any of the major coastal checkpoints and the required rest has been increased to six hours.)

"This is it. The last leg of the race, about 75 miles to Front Street. It's 3 a.m. and I'm amazed at what four hours of rest has done for my team. I think back to the Beargrease this past January, where we left another four-hour mandatory layover bound for the finish line—left it by inchworming the entire team up the hill and finally got them underway with sharp words and a lot of false optimism. Leaving White Mountain, there is none of that. I shout their names and urge them to their feet; they get up and trot down the trail. Now we're away from the river and climbing into some treeless hills. They're moving steadily and looking a lot perkier than I feel. There's barely any snow here. It looks as though the race will finish with the nerve-wracking rasp of sled runners on bare ground. Appropriate, this year."

I remember stopping for a 20-minute break at about 4:30 a.m., giving the dogs a snack and going back to sit on the sled. When I woke it was 5:45 a.m. Angry, cold and confused, I roused the team and we got underway again.

At this point in the race, the pressure of racing had dwindled to nothing for me. It was clear where we would finish—there was no one ahead whom we could catch and there was no one hell-bent on catching us.

We would not finish in the money and about the only strong incentive to push hard that day was to make Nome in time for the banquet that night at 7 p.m. I had to laugh aloud at that—some people will do anything for a free meal.

My mood was calm at last and appreciative of that last stretch of the Iditarod Trail. We climbed steadily up and over bare hills to the summit of Topkok Head. The notorious windblown draw near Topkok was calm and clear that morning as we passed through just after dawn.

I remember stopping on a high crest just before Topkok to watch the sun clear the hills to the east. It was only five days until the vernal equinox. I felt at ease in the country by then—not like I do in the Canadian North, where I have spent more time, but comfortable and ready to face whatever might happen along the trail.

The trail drops from Topkok Head in a dramatic descent to the shoreline of the Bering Sea. From there, it is a straight 35 miles or so to the checkpoint at Port Safety. This stretch was sandy and rocky and there was not enough snow anywhere for good sledding, but after a final fit of frustration I found a decent trail of icy ruts and we made reasonable time. By 2 p.m. we were at Safety Roadhouse.

I fed the dogs a little bit there and offered them some water. I gave most of my non-mandatory gear to a family from Nome who had offered to take it to town. I pulled out at about 3 p.m. with the lightest load I'd had in the sled for the entire race. It was warm and sunny. There was no wind and the dogs were willing only to float along in a halfhearted trot.

The trail in 1986 had been routed up and around the back side of Cape Nome, adding five miles to the traditional 22 from Safety to the finish line. We climbed, the sun beat down and gradually a few tuglines went slack.

I cajoled, sang, growled a little and pedaled up the hills. Beaver, Jake and Grayling—those were the three that had what it took that afternoon. The rest of them, for most of that last three hours, were just in the team for looks. I had dropped Henry in Safety.

"There are seven dogs in my team and we're going home. Just cresting the hill behind town and I can see antennas, a few buildings and a road. Mike Jackson has come out in the KNOM radio car to see me in. He knows John Bauman and suddenly I think of John on Mount Logan and wonder if they've made it. They've got a few days left to complete a winter ascent. The dogs drift toward the road where a pickup is parked, a family inside taking pictures of us.

"A warm, calm Sunday evening—only a few miles to go . . . Now we're along the beach, somebody calls out 'Welcome to Fort Davis!' and I laugh. The dogs are just floating, tongues out, strides long and loose, nobody taking much credit for the fact that the sled continues to move forward. . .

"And now the town siren goes off, as we climb onto Front Street itself. 'Straight ahead, you guys, on by.' Down the main street, past the stores and bars and houses of this biggest town we've seen since Anchorage. 'Let's go home. . .' "

The finish was much like that entire last leg—quiet and contemplative. Almost everyone in town was over at the banquet hall, where the festivities were to begin in 20 minutes. Like every arriving musher, I was greeted by the mayor of Nome after someone went and found him and I talked with the reporter from KNOM radio. I don't remember a word that I said. A crew from the dog lot hustled my team out of the chute and into the holding area as Steve Bush came onto Front Street. I thought about trying to track down my food supplies, but I knew that all those dogs really wanted to do that evening was sleep. I would feed them after a few hours— if I could wake them up! They curled up on mounds of clean straw in the huge dog lot and I climbed into Mike's car for a ride to the banquet.

We finished 31st in a field of 73 starters and 55 finishers. Our official time was 15 days, 9 hours, 44 minutes and 15 seconds. That night at the banquet, I was given the Sportsmanship Award for my actions on behalf of Bill Cowart just out of Rohn checkpoint.

The banquet was, as always, a rousing celebration and I dozed only once during it. Dirty, windburned and unshaven, I sat with Pete Sapin and Mike Senty from Grand Marais and enjoyed the party.

When it was over, I went out to tend and feed my dogs. They all seemed to sense, then, that we were at the end of the trail and I assured them that we wouldn't be sledding out of this checkpoint.

I walked to the house where I was to stay, took a shower and fell asleep. Every few hours, I would wake up, panic, realize gradually where I was and fall back to sleep. . . . Nome, sweet Nome.

From my journal, March 20, 1986, Knik, Alaska:

"It's over. Iditarod '86 is all memories and a mound of smelly harnesses and clothing, a torn sled bag, shredded dog booties, half-dead D batteries. . . . Arrived in Anchorage yesterday on Alaska Airlines, a 737 from Nome, via Kotzebue.

"It was all I'd ever dreamt it would be and more and less and different from those dreams. I laughed, sang, cursed, commiserated, sweated, shivered and stumbled 1,200 miles across the 'mountains and rivers without end' that are Alaska. Brought 14 dogs clear to the coast and seven of them to Nome. Now the team is all together again, tied out around the truck, sleeping, wrestling with each other, eating and happily barking.

"Out on the trail I made mistakes—running when I should have been resting, resting when I should have been running, not caring well enough for my dogs, their feet, their food, their mood and spirit.

"*The trail was bad, perhaps the most physically punishing Iditarod yet, with no snow in many stretches—glare ice, gravel, grass, sand—and crusty paw-tearing corn snow for miles.*

"*I fell behind, helping another musher, getting lost again and again, rewiring my headlamp, struggling with my cookstove—rookie moves.*

"*Now I have rejoined my friends, back in the crowded basement where we'd made our base camp before the race. Sifting through equipment, news clips, notebook pages filled with lists, tattered receipts from the many expenditures, my mind wanders ahead—will I do this again? When? How? Why?*

"*I tire of the cheapened hype of the race—mushers depicted as 'the heroes of the north . . . the hardy and the brave . . . the daring breed' and so on,* ad nauseum. *The running of this race is an endeavor with its own kind of nobility, apart from the corny heroism of the press reports. The Iditarod Trail is demanding and rewarding. It demands humility and tenacity. It offers moments of terror, serenity and beauty. As veteran musher Jerry Austin put it at the final banquet, we must try to bring together these four:* patience, perseverance, pride *and* performance.

"*Now I look ahead, to the long road south and east, the return to friends and family, flying, puppies, to a hangar full of piled-up belongings, to a summer filled with work and preparations for another journey north and west.*

"*And behind, to moments I'll never forget: the clarity of sunlight on Alaskan peaks, numbing cold on the Yukon River, the bizarre daze of fatigue on a moonless night along the coast of the Bering Sea. On and on . . . a full 1,200 miles in 15 days.*

"*Never again will my dogs and I be rookies on the Iditarod Trail.*"

HALF BROTHERS

SOMETIMES IT'S HEAVEN AND SOMETIMES IT'S NOT AND that afternoon on the west end of Campbell Lake was a slice of pure heaven for us. It was April 20, 1981, and it was lunchtime. Kurt Mitchell and I were hunkered down on the leeward side of our overloaded freight sled, eagerly gnawing huge chunks of frozen Logan bread and swilling cup after cup of hot tea. We were westbound, toward Reliance, in a headlong retreat after an aborted crossing of the barrenlands to Baker Lake. Over the past five weeks we had battled with storms, deep snow, our own mistakes and shortcomings and a serious lack of adequate dog power. "That's life on the tundra" had become our catch-all phrase, an arctic equivalent to Murphy's Law.

But that day—that day was something else again. The sun was warm and the brilliant glare of the springtime barrens extended away from the lake in all directions. For three days we had seen no sign of another living creature. We were alone in one of North America's loneliest neighborhoods.

Then, for no apparent reason, one of our dogs barked. At about the same moment the sled, our backrest,

157

was yanked out from behind us. I tipped over into the trail, sloshing hot tea down the front of my parka.

"What the. . ."

"Wolf!"

Kurt was up and running. The sled was moving, towed by our ten dogs, and they were pulling away from us. Ahead of Turok and Mukluk, 30 feet north of the team, trotted a pure white 70-to 80-pound wolf. I leapt to my feet, still spluttering tea and crumbs, and raced behind Kurt after the runaway sled. The dogs barked insanely as they ran. Suddenly the wolf wheeled and stopped. The team fell into a pile in a sudden effort to slow down and we pitched the top-heavy sled over on its side.

For a moment, no one moved. The dogs stood, we sat on the overturned sled and the wolf stared back at us all. Then she turned and trotted away again. Sinker ventured a bark. Mukluk turned her wise old gaze on him as if to say, "Shut up, you idiot!" The wolf moved off further—100 feet, 200—then stopped and turned and stared again. Kurt, a professional photographer, was just sitting there, soaking it all in. Some moments are impossible to capture on film.

Like a ghost, that white wolf slowly evaporated into the white world of the barrens. Her black nose when she turned and the black pads on her paws as she sauntered slowly away were the last things to disappear. I walked back to our scattered lunch, salvaged what I could for us and we sat down to finish our interrupted rest break. After five minutes the dogs were all sound asleep—all except Sinker, who evidently figured he didn't want to risk being surprised like *that* again. He sat up, alert and eagerly sniffing the breeze, until we started west.

Wolves and dogs. Dogs and wolves. *Canis lupus, Canis familiaris.* Some taxonomists once wanted to break down those distinctions. Dogs are wolves, they claimed. The species distinction is contrived for the comfort of us humans who have so long loved our selected mutant strains of wolves, our "dogs."

This makes sense to anyone who has been fortunate enough to watch wolves in their natural habitat, or in a fairly unrestricted confinement. Watching their patterns of behavior, one is immediately struck by their "dog-like" movements and mannerisms. To be more precise, though, we should say that the "wolf-like" behavior of dogs is what is so striking. The wolf came first and from the wolf, the dogs—all dogs. It is easier to accept the wolfish ancestry of Man's best friend if one is looking at sled dogs, German shepherds, or even Labrador retrievers, but the fact is that even the chihuahuas, the dachshunds and the little Lhasa apsos are descendants of—and in many ways still *are*—wolves. Selective breeding, occasional mutations and genetic diversity account for the differences.

Running sled dogs, on trips and courses and training trails and races, almost always in prime wolf habitat from northern Minnesota to Great Slave Lake, has brought me into contact with these half brothers of my dogs in some memorable, dramatic ways.

One cold morning in November 1986, I was running a team of nine dogs on a 30-mile training loop across the ice of Granville Lake, Manitoba. Ahead of me, Mike Dietzman had eight dogs in his team. The wind was bitter that day and we were both submerged as far as we could get into the cinched-up ruffs of our parkas. I think I was staring at my sled's brush bow, lost in thought, something I tend to do on long windy training runs, when I felt that unmistakable surge of power that comes up through the soles of one's mukluks and the handlebar of the sled and that can mean only one thing—the dogs have sensed something interesting ahead and they are in hot pursuit.

I looked up and could hardly believe my eyes. If I had been out on a long, sleepless race, I might have chalked the whole scene up to hallucination. But I was well-rested and there they were—wolves. Not a couple, not half a dozen, but wolves, it seemed, everywhere I looked.

The huge pack—I counted 14 once I regained my composure—was evidently as surprised as we were by the encounter. They were scattering in all directions, the dogs were yipping and galloping and had turned completely away from our trail. Up ahead, oblivious to it all, Mike and his dogs were just trotting out of sight around a point.

The ice on Granville that day was smooth and black and the snow cover had been blown off almost completely in wide patches. I gave my leaders, Julie and Grayling, my most casual "whoa" as I tried to set the snowhook into any available flaw in the surface of the ice. The wolves had divided into two groups of six and eight and all but two of them had reached either a large island or the mainland. But those last two, big tawny fellows, had turned and now stood their ground, watching the dogs approach.

The dogs were less and less enthusiastic about this chase as they drew closer to the two big wolves. They started sending furtive glances over their shoulders, plainly saying, "Just give us the word, chief, and we're out of here." Finally, the points of my snowhook snagged a meandering crack in the ice and we jerked to a stop. The wolves began to trot away from us, turning every few steps to watch us, just as the lone white wolf on the barrens had done.

As I carefully moved forward alongside my team and began to swing the leaders around, someone back in the ranks decided to give one more little lunge. I felt the team begin to move ahead and I assumed that they had popped the snowhook loose. They had. But the bridle loop on the sled had also popped, there was no convenient handlebar for me to catch and soon my team was veering away, back toward the wolves, towing only a snubline and a snowhook.

The wolves stopped again and turned toward us. As nonchalantly as I could, I scampered up behind the team and dived on the snowhook as if it were a fumbled ball in the Super Bowl.

I sat there then, on the ice, talking softly to the dogs and suddenly through my thick fur earflaps and parka hood came the sound of a chorus of wolves, howling in stereo from the island on the right and the mainland back to the left. That, perhaps, was a signal to the two males in the rear guard. With an air of decisiveness, they trotted swiftly onto the wooded island and disappeared. I rejoined dogteam to sled, turned back to the trail and we moved on to catch up with Dietz.

He did not quite believe my story until he saw all the tracks.

Keeping a team of sled dogs, for anyone with an interest in wolves, is about the next best thing to having intimate, daily contact with a wild pack. Many of the social intricacies that biologists have begun to recognize and delineate among wolves are present in the dog yard. There are "alpha" animals—the leaders of the pack. In a dogteam, these are not necessarily the same as the lead dogs, though they can be. They are the king and queen, to whom the rest of the dogs almost always defer.

Of course, with the dogs confined to their circles and stakes outdoors, or to their stalls in a barn, the interactions between them are limited and modified. But in a remote setting like our homestead, where the entire "pack" can run free occasionally, the team does develop a discernible hierarchy.

In recent years we have bought very few new dogs, so increasingly the dogs in our kennel are all directly related. The puppies at eight weeks or so begin to cautiously make their way into the dog yard, meeting a single adult at a time, one to one. They make obsequious gestures of submission as they approach each adult, creeping in on their bellies, rolling over in complete surrender and licking at the muzzles of the adults. All of these behaviors can be seen among wolf packs, which are also extended family units.

Though the wolf ancestry of the neighborhood terrier may seem farfetched, the wolf ancestry of most sled dogs is obvious. This is especially true in the teams of larger, less "racy" dogs still found at work on traplines and in remote northern villages. The build of those dogs, their gait and posture, their color patterns and thick coats, all link them directly to their wild brothers. In fact, in many working teams from Greenland to Alaska, there are dog-wolf hybrids that have resulted either from chance encounters or planned matings.

Mushers speculate endlessly on the pros and cons of such crosses, but these days there seems to be a consensus that there is little to be gained from such breedings. As a friend of mine remarked, "There's now so much good blood available *as sled dogs* that there's no use stepping backward and trying to reinvent the breed." True, I think, but the prospect does provide good fodder for late-night conversation.

In central Alaska years ago, there was a line of sled dogs that became known as "Johnny Allen dogs." They were reputed to be one quarter setter, one quarter wolf and one half Siberian. One physical feature that identified them was a black spot on the tongue. In 1987, at the end of the Iditarod race in Nome, I bought a female dog named Rajah from musher Gary Guy, who lives in Galena on the Yukon River. She was a husky's husky—tough and wiry, with "steel-belted" feet and a flying trot. One warm day after a training run, I noticed her panting hard as she waited to be taken out of harness. Sure enough— a big black splotch of pigmented skin was in the center of her bright pink tongue. Since then, she has been my "Johnny Allen bitch," and thus "part wolf," to anyone willing to put up with my babbling. Her gait, her eyes and her markings certainly are reminiscent of wolves. Admittedly, though, mushers can *see* almost any trait in a dog once we convince ourselves we want it to be there.

I once spent some time with a captive wolf named Esker who was being kept with a team of sled dogs. From the age of ten days she had been partially socialized to humans and completely accepted by dogs. At first glance she looked like a large husky, but there were differences. One that I will never forget was that her jaws were far more powerful than those of the average sled dog. To hear them slam shut on a bit of meat tossed into the air was enough to make me shudder. *That* was power—a kind of power that our domesticated dogs with their prepared diets no longer needed.

There was something else, a look in her eye and a certain stance, that set that wolf apart from the dogs. She had a way of meeting a person's eyes and holding them, like the subject's eyes do in certain painted portraits. She would drop her head slightly and gaze at a newcomer, not in submission, but in judgment. She was sizing the stranger up, it seemed—for physical traits, yes, but more for integrity, for trustworthiness. Her gaze was different from the open, eager-to-please looks of the dogs. She was a wolf and a wolf she always remained.

As she grew up, I could not resist the temptation to try Esker out in harness, if only as a way to give her some exercise and let her roam a bit—something she could not be allowed to do on her own. So for days and weeks at a stretch, I would lead her over to the wheel-dog position in a small team, ease her into a harness and slowly, smoothly back away. I would step on the sled and off the team would go—three or four dogs and a tall ungainly wolf.

She learned to run in a team that spring, but I would be exaggerating if I claimed that she learned to pull, or ever truly relaxed and enjoyed the runs. She was immensely strong, like a fur-covered coil of spring steel, and there were a few moments during her time in harness when I was convinced she was happy. It was a thrill to watch her move down the trail ahead of the sled and to let my mind wander back across thousands of years to the ancient roots of sled dog and musher.

In 1986 I worked as a pilot for a government study of the timber wolves in northern Minnesota. Day after day, through all seasons of the year, we flew out over the lakes and forests as the biologist tracked the tiny radio transmitters that hung in collars around the wolves' necks. Often on those flights, we would watch a pack traveling in single file along a logging road or a frozen creek. As we circled above them, it was easy for me to imagine the six or eight of them harnessed together in a team, pulling a trapper along his trail. They had a loose, forward-reaching trot that looked almost floppy in the wrist joints. Their feet, in comparison to those of sled dogs, looked like snowshoes.

When the biologist needed to make notes on a specific wolf, we would sometimes make a low pass at a pack as they crossed a lake. They would scatter with astonishing quickness, putting on a burst of speed that was as hard to believe as it would have been to measure. They would sometimes run in a wild zigzag pattern, as if expecting to be gunned down from above at any moment.

This raises a key point in the idle comparisons of wolf speeds to dog speeds. Experienced hunters and trappers and reputable biologists report some staggering flat-out speeds for wolves, faster than the fastest sprint sled dogs—upwards of 40 miles per hour. This makes me wonder how fast the fastest sled dogs could travel if they were running free and were convinced somehow that their *lives* were on the line. They would run at least as fast, I think, and probably could hold their speed much farther than those 70- to 100-pound wolves. More material for late-night speculation.

Often wolves approach a wilderness camp or cabin where dogs are kept. Their motives are not easy to understand or predict, but their actions can sometimes speak all too clearly. Although healthy, unprovoked wolves have never attacked a human being in North America, the same cannot be said of their relationship with our dogs. Rare and unlucky mushers from Minnesota to Alaska have come out to their dog yards on a winter morning to find only the remains of a dog and signs of a brief, bloody skirmish. Perhaps there is a territorial motive beyond simple hunger and predation, but I am no scientist and the subject is complex. Each situation is different.

When I lived for part of a winter in a tent camp near Ely, Minnesota, I would often return after a week's absence to find the snow around my camp trampled by wolf tracks. They had sniffed and explored every corner of the dog yard (the dogs having been away with me), every tree and woodpile and tent pole had been sprayed with urine and any scraps of fat or meat from the dog's food were gone. I wished I could somehow have watched them while they carefully and thoroughly explored our camp.

A mushing family in northern Manitoba, Bill and Shirley Hicks and their children, keep their dogs in a fenced compound on the outskirts of Leaf Rapids. Their kennel is impressive—clean, organized and well-built. Since all the dogs are staked out on chains within the compound, each with a house, I asked Bill once why he had gone to the trouble of erecting a fence. "Wolves," he said. "They'd come right in and clean me out." At the time, I didn't quite believe him. I think he realized that and he proceeded to tell me some chilling stories of pups and dogs who had literally had their faces torn off when they poked their noses out through the fence to greet a visiting wolf.

At the Voyageur Outward Bound School where my dogs and I worked for several winters, there was a wolf who came around the dog yard regularly. Evidently the biologists at the nearby research center knew her well, calling her by the number of her radio transmitter. She was an old female, they said, and toothless. She would come by and clean up all the dog food scraps in the snow around the yard. The dogs seemed almost to like her; they at least tolerated her nightly foraging. She had found what she needed—a source of food that did not need to be torn from a carcass with sharp teeth. We joked about buying her dentures and Poly-Grip for Christmas. I was told that she did not make it through that winter, but her death was probably not from starvation.

One November I spent several cold, restless nights at our Churchill River camp, bivouacked down along the dog's picket line, a rifle and a headlamp within reach next to my sleeping bag. We had heard the dogs carrying on, howling and barking excitedly, for several nights in a row and the tracks one morning told the story of two wolves who had come within five feet of one end of the picket line. There was a female in heat there, Makepeace and a cluster of yearling dogs around her. We were not sure if the visitors had strolled by in search of love or lunch.

After three nights camped out with the dogs, I decided to take the advice Bill Hicks had given us. We erected full-scale scarecrows made of old clothes and spruce branches at each end of the dog yard and doused them every morning with the contents of our cabin's piss can. The tracks did not reappear; the howling and night-long barking ceased.

The east end of Great Slave Lake and the barrens north and east from there are the territory of some of the most wide-ranging and physically striking races of wolves. These are the tundra wolves, or caribou wolves, whose lives are intrinsically bound to the wandering herds of barren-ground caribou. These wolves are often nearly pure white and in build they are leggy and tall and immensely powerful.

At the Hoarfrost River, training and keeping our kennel of sled dogs, we are often aware of the presence of these magnificent wolves. Also, our friends and neighbors depend on a harvest of some wolves each winter as a part of their hunting and trapping livelihood. Wolf sightings and stories are central to the lore of the country.

It's time to elaborate on the people who make their living in the northern wilderness, harvesting—and by that I mean killing—fur-bearing animals. They, the hunters and trappers of the north, have had by far the most long-standing and consistent involvement with sled dogs of any group of mushers. To mention them only in passing might be construed as purposeful avoidance of what has recently become a controversial topic.

For thousands of years, human life in the northern reaches of the world has been a life of hunting, of predation, of harvesting living animals for their meat, their hides, their bones and fat. It is simplistic and naïve, but all too easy, to pronounce that "those days are over," that the life of the hunter and trapper is and should be, doomed to extinction.

Consider for a moment the outcome of such a change in the North. In an ecosystem totally dependent on the few animals, such as caribou, that can convert the land's sparse vegetation into protein and sustenance for humans and other predators, is there not a place, in fact a *need*, for humans *and* other predators? Or shall the North become simply the domain of the passing tourist, the prospector and the large-scale mineral developer—a vast, silent land where no human being permanently *lives*?

Hunters and trappers live as true *inhabitants* of their ecosystems, or as nearly so as modern people seem to be capable of living. In ways as simple and obvious as they are powerful, they are physically tied to the land, to "the country," as they often call it. Though they take life from it, they also give life back to it, in a vital and tangible way. *They live in a place,* and are bound up with its cycles and creatures, season after season, year after year. I believe that the world would be poorer and a great wealth of lore and understanding would be lost if we forced from the northern wilderness those individuals who so directly devote their lives to it.

A parka ruff of wolf fur, mukluks sewn of sealskin, or mitts made from the hide of a moose—these are honest, direct attachments to the life and death cycles of the world. No polyester garments, no Polarfleece or Thinsulate or even cotton denim come to us without dramatic effect on the global ecosystem. If there is a place for human use within the balances of caribou, wolves, foxes and wolverines, as astute and appreciative biologists assure us there is, then those people who choose to pursue this life should be accepted, admired, listened to and learned from. They possess an understanding, an awareness of wilderness in all its facets that is rare and endangered.

Back to the team's half brothers of the tundra and treeline. They are our most vocal neighbors here. Often in the morning darkness of winter, the dogs will suddenly join in a long chorus of howls. As their wails end, we listen and somewhere in the distance can be heard the singing of wolves. We pass their tracks on our training runs and sometimes see them ahead of us, on the ice of Great Slave or on smaller lakes to the north. But rarely, in this country of skillful hunters and trappers, do they come close to our home and dog yard.

One night in mid-January 1988, I was in bed reading a book. It was one of the coldest nights of the winter, −52 degrees to be exact. The dogs had not run that day and they were all asleep outdoors in their tiny wooden houses. I had given them an extra feeding of fat just before going to bed. I was concerned for them. Such temperatures take their toll even on hardy, heavily furred dogs.

All at once, there was a tremendous racket from the dog yard. Everyone was barking and I was certain that they had seen something moving in the woods, or that one of them was running free. Such noise on such a cold night is not a pleasant sound to the ears of a dog musher. At first there is the lazy inclination to ignore the commotion and hope that it will abruptly end. But it almost never does, until one has bundled up and gone out to investigate. That night, for some reason, it sounded to me like there was more than a loose dog or a foraging weasel to blame. So, as I stumbled outside in my long-johns, cap, mukluks and gloves, I paused in the storm porch to strap on a headlamp and reached for the rifle that was hanging above the door.

Chaos prevailed in the dog yard. Nearly everyone was up on their house or tearing in circles around their poles, all barking and staring off to the far edge of the cluster of stakes and houses. I switched on the powerful beam of the headlamp and scanned the yard. The retinas in the eyes of every dog shone back at me—greens, blues, a few reds—all blinking in the bright glare as the light passed across them. And there, beyond Julie and Fletcher, was another pair of eyes, deep blue and glassy in their sparkle, slightly more widely spaced than those of my dogs, shining back at me. No dog was staked out there, just behind our compost pile of kitchen scraps, sawdust and dog yard tailings.

I paused to count, remembering stories of mushers who had mistakenly shot their own loose dogs in the confusion, darkness and cold of a winter's night. The dogs were all in their places; no one was loose. Fletcher, a young dog then, was on the far side of the yard. He hung back from the visitor, not barking, and glanced at me nervously. Julie, who was next to Fletcher and closest to the edge of the kennel, was in heat. She sat just inside her little house, peering back and forth, from me to what I knew by then was a wolf.

With my light I scanned the sparse spruce woods down toward the lakeshore, looking for more eyes but seeing none. I was shivering and the deep cold bit through my woolen longjohns and nipped the tip of my nose. I turned the headlamp to the side of my hat and raised the rifle so that the beam of the light still captured those two blue eyes above the post of the gunsight.

There was no long soul-searching decision that night for me. This wolf was too close to my animals and I knew quite well what might happen over the course of the long night. I squeezed the trigger, a sharp crack sounded and the wolf fell. The dogs were instantly silent. I walked forward. The wolf did not move. The .22 magnum bullet had gone into its left eye and on through its brain.

As I dragged the carcass back across the yard to the cabin, I was shocked at its emaciated condition, in a year when most wolves were fat with the abundant caribou of the country. I hung it in the porch and the next morning I carefully examined it before my trapper friends arrived to show me how to skin it. Seven feet, three inches, from the tip of the nose to the tip of the tail—a tall white male with a black stripe down the center of his back. The paws were huge, with tough black pads that would be the envy of any Iditarod husky. It was a beautiful animal, but it had been suffering from some chronic and debilitating condition. Its backbone and pelvis protruded sharply through its luxurious pelt. It was a walking skeleton in a thick fur coat. Worms, perhaps, or some prolonged disease had robbed it of all traces of extra flesh.

I tell this story because that night held a clear lesson for me about the keeping of domestic animals and about the essence that separates dogs from wolves. The dogs are totally dependent upon us—for food, for shelter and for protection. Abandoned in the wild, most of them would soon be killed, or would starve. The wolves, on the other hand, are totally independent of us. If they cross the line, driven by disease or desperation, and try to enter our world, they are soon killed. Yet the strange connection, the kinship of wolf and northern dog, survives. I respected and appreciated that wolf, the wild spirit he embodied, even as I killed him. Perhaps some people cannot understand that or accept my actions.

In late winter, the female wolves come into estrus. The caribou are on the move, the wolf packs are traveling with them, the days are lengthening and the whole landscape is coming back to life. Often on those days in March, a group of wolves will rest offshore, a mile or two out on the ice of the big lake. In the bright sunshine they sit or even lie down, tip their heads back and howl. The dogs in the yard here gaze out at the lake, ears tilted forward, and one by one join the wavering chorus that floats on the clear, cool air. Back and forth, hour after hour, they call and answer each other, these half brothers.

SUMMER CAMP

"P ARIAH"—THAT ONE SENT ME TO THE DICTIONARY.
My friend Randy Crawford, always one for the right
word, remarked to me one day that he considered sled
dogs in the summer to be pariahs. A pariah, I found out
from Mr. Webster, is "any outcast; someone despised or
rejected by others." Though it seemed to be a bit of an
overstatement to apply that term to my dogs, I had to
admit that the underlying feeling was about right at
times, in the heat and rain and bugs of midsummer. I
thought of the word as I walked past my long line of
dogs that night, down the hill to my old Airstream trailer
with its leaky roof and constant odor of mildew. It was
a warm humid night just before a July thunderstorm and
the dogs watched me walk past with looks of bored res-
ignation.

Sled dogs in summer are creatures only a musher
can love. Gone is their thick glossy pelage of winter,
their robust hardness after thousands of miles of running,
their cleanliness in the cold sterility of snow and ice.
They shed, they roll in the sand or romp in the mud,
they get bitten by flies and the odor of strong urine and

unfrozen manure hangs in the air of the dog yard no matter how fastidiously we scoop and spray and pamper. On some days, "pariah" seems all too accurate.

I will admit to having kept some kennels over the years that should by rights have landed me in jail, facing a firing squad manned by the local humane society. My dogs have for days at a time endured mud, slop and filth of ungodly magnitude. My only plea has been that I have not fared much better during those times. During one of the rainiest autumns the Boundary Waters ever had, my team and I were camped in a muddy clearing near Isabella, Minnesota. No one, including the musher, had a proper house that fall. We were all wet, muddy, cold and generally disgusting for days at a stretch. But we survived; the dogs were fed each day with good food, they were running in harness and gaining in strength and when winter finally came with snow and cold weather and long, fast runs, none of us were suffering any ill effects.

By comparison, my summer dog yard now is as nearly perfect as I could ever imagine. It is August 8 and it has been a cold, rainy summer. Today the dogs are all sprawled in the loose sand of their yard or atop their wooden houses as a cool, dry breeze flows out of the west. This morning I turned them all free and they pounded up and down the beach between our homestead and the river mouth at a flat-out gallop. With their tongues sailing off to one side of their open mouths, they splashed up to their thighs in the cold clear water of Great Slave, growled and sniffed and harassed each other and came happily back to their circles when I called them. None of them can remember those past summers in temporary quarters, in the jungles of northern Minnesota, but I can and I know we have come at last to the right part of the world.

My dogs last ran on the lake ice on the second of June, hauling firewood across the inlet from the shoreline east of here. Since then, they have spent the vast majority

of their time tethered to their stakes and for an unbe-
lievable proportion of each day they have all been sound
asleep. I am always astounded at the capacity dogs have
for sleep and in summer they indulge it to the fullest.
Each night they are fed, precisely at 10:15 on these endless northern evenings. Every morning I clean the yard
with a shovel and bucket, haul fresh water to each dog,
feed the puppies and, when conditions warrant, spray
everyone with an insect repellent developed for use on
horses. When the mood strikes me, I let them all run
free, or harness a few of them to a weighted toboggan
for some pulling practice on the beach.

But all in all, I leave the dogs alone. The brief weeks
of summer pass. This is the off-season—a time for any of
their nagging muscular aches and pains to slowly and
completely mend. It is a time for constructing new buildings, tanning a moose hide, visiting with friends, fishing
and swimming and berry picking. It is also a time for
remembering that life, at least for us humans, does not
begin and end in the dog yard. No longer do I dread the
summer, even with so many dogs to care for.

The far north is a marvelous place to keep sled dogs,
but I do not want to give the impression that all sled dog
kennels further to the south are squalid and unkempt in
the off-season. My own problem, when I lived down
there, was simply one of transience. I owned no place of
my own and my dogs and I were too frequently pulling
up and putting down stakes, literally. With time and
planning and proper care, a sled dog team can summer
happily in almost any location.

Most of the non-mushing public must assume that
dog teams miraculously appear from nowhere with the
start of winter and the first snowfall. Summer visitors to
our kennel often greet the dogs with a kind of surprised
bewilderment, as if they had completely forgotten that
the team *existed* apart from sleds and snow and trips and
races. Their comments are predictable. "The dogs must
really tie you down, huh?" "No fun having dogs in the

summer, eh?" "Guess you can't just park these things in the garage when the snow melts, can you?"

Certainly, there are days when my dogs feel like a burden to me, when I question my goals and progress and my desire to go on with this mushing life. But the dogs are nearly second nature to me now. They are a part of the daily round and the chores and limitations and concerns they represent are balanced by the freedom and travel and excitement they make possible. I do not envy my footloose, fancy-free, dogless friends any more *often* than some of them envy the special attachment and commitment I have to my dogteam. You get what you pay for.

Summer brings changes to the dog yard. The dogs all shed their thick winter coats and for a few weeks or a month the entire kennel is awash in loose, dingy underfur. The dogs look their worst as they "blow their coats," with ragged wisps of hair hanging from their legs and backs and bellies. I have heard about mushers who brush all their dogs to hurry them through this phase. Those people must have *plenty* of time on their hands!

After they shed, the dogs all look much leaner than they have all winter. I think this accounts in part for the persistent notion that sled dogs all get "thinned down" (some say "half-starved") over the summer months. No serious dog musher ever wants his or her dogs to become either underweight or overweight, in *any* season of the year. It does take slightly less food to maintain an animal, any animal, in warmer weather, but only a fool would claim that there was any logic in starving the dogs over the summer only to fatten them up again in the fall.

It is always amazing to me to walk past my dogs after they have shed and see the lean physiques that have been so long hidden beneath thick fur. Amazing and inspiring, since by late summer they all look like the marathon runners they are.

Summer is also the season of puppies and breedings. Careful planning goes into the matings that are desired each year and every breeding bitch is watched closely for signs that she will soon be fertile. Most bitches cycle on about a six-month period, but some seem to be easily thrown off schedule by other females, nearby males and other factors that no one yet understands. By timing the breedings for summer births, the pups come into the world at its warmest and easiest season and the bitches have time to recover from the stress of pregnancy and motherhood before they begin training for the coming winter.

In the days of complete dependence upon dogs for northern winter transportation, the teams were smaller than the competitive teams of today. A trapper might have half a dozen big dogs and would feed them over the summer by netting fish, shooting game, or—in dire times—cooking oatmeal or rice "straight up" for them.

In the days before airplanes, hunters and trappers and their dogs had to set out for their winter camps long before the coming of snow and ice. The dogs would follow along the shores of the lakes and rivers, crashing through the brush in a desperate effort to keep pace with the canoe or riverboat or barge.

Whenever there was a load to be hauled overland, the dogs were hard at work again, straining under pack-sacks attached like saddlebags to their backs, across hills and mountain passes and long expanses of tundra. In those days, there was little concern over a gradual loss of the dogs' endurance over the summer!

In the modern kennels of the elite, champion mushers, it is common to see an ungainly apparatus known as a "hot walker," or simply a "walker." This is a giant carousel, like the pony-ride rig at the carnival, with either a motor or a set of friction gears at its center. Long metal poles extend out like spokes from the hub and to these the dogs' collars are attached by short leads. They walk or run in a wide circle, at a pace controlled by the motor or by friction. Thus their muscle tone and condition can be efficiently maintained. I have yet to see one of these contraptions in action, but they seem to be the coming rage among competitive mushers.

A few years ago, Ed Dallas of Minnesota unveiled his "Doggie-Dyno" treadmill. I never saw that one underway either, but it did prompt some imagined scenarios that we chuckled over for a long time—dog musher indoors, watching T.V., sipping a cold beer, fully harnessed ten-dog team outside the window logging miles on the treadmill. . . . Perhaps we were just jealous.

All in all, though, I still enjoy the simple, apparatus-free summer exercise that my team gets, sprinting up and down the beach and splashing through the shallows. There is no worry about the dogs bothering our nearest neighbors, who are separated from us by 11 miles of 40-degree water.

No discussion of northern summer and northern sled dogs in that season would be complete without mention of the bugs: mosquitoes, blackflies or sandflies, deer flies, "bulldogs," "no-see-ums," the works. For the musher and team caught unprepared, these hordes can be almost life-threatening in their ferocity. Smudge pots and coils, creams and repellents, impregnated collars and screened barns are among the effective tactics used to fight this all-important summer battle.

The old-time mushers in the Northwest Territories are said to have favored a liberal dose of used crankcase oil on the dogs' heads and bellies. Around Will Steger's place a favorite method of combatting the biting flies was a thick coat of brightly colored latex paste that completely encapsulated the vulnerable tips of the dogs' ears. The bugs are the price we pay, all across the north, for the long hours of daylight, the warm, windless weather and the abundant standing and running water. On some days we pay in full, in blood.

Summer is the time when a musher takes time to step back from the day-to-day effort of training and racing and caring for a team. It is the season when we can take a long view and try to comprehend where the team stands and where it is headed. I often rush in to my desk after a round of morning chores in mid-July, pull off my work gloves and fill an entire sheet of looseleaf paper with scribbled lists of dogs and notes—name, age, sex, experience, potential. I am sizing up the roster for the coming season.

It is easy to lose sight of the big picture amidst the demands of a busy winter. Summer is the time to stand still at the edge of the yard late in the evening and mull over each individual dog. Who will be coming on strong next season? Who is getting close to retirement age? What is happening in this team, overall, over time? Are they getting any faster, any tougher, any bigger or smaller in average size? Sometimes months can pass when I do not pause and *think* about such things. Summer is a good season for such reflection.

The off-season is also the time to consider another aspect of the big picture—dollars. Keeping a team of dogs, 10 or 20 or 50 in a yard, involves more than a few expenses. The expense that non-mushers most often harp upon and wonder over is actually among the least of the concerns—the actual daily cost of feeding the team. Adequate dog food, capable of sustaining the average dog in average activity, is easily accessible in almost every corner of North America and available at a reasonable cost. It is not the cost of maintenance, but instead the efforts to *enhance* the dogs' diet, to *increase* strength and endurance, to *improve* the quality of training and traveling that bring kennel budgets to staggering sums. It is when a musher and a team begin to strive for something beyond the average and ordinary that money becomes a major concern.

Without institutional and corporate sponsorship of both individual teams and entire races, the sport of sled dog racing would be dead. Sponsorship, the provision of material or financial support, is part of the lifeblood of competitive mushing. Whether the sponsor is a mom-and-pop grocery store backing the local novice or Alaska

179

Airlines underwriting some of the costs and logistics of the Iditarod Trail race, the support is vital.

Dog mushing is a sport that has not hit the big time. This might sound surprising to someone in Alaska, who after three solid weeks of hourly media "updates" on the Yukon Quest and Iditarod begins to *wish* the events were obscure. When compared to other professional sports, though, like horse racing or golf or even bowling, the prize money, spectator numbers and press coverage of dog mushing are infinitesimal.

I have often been chagrined by the response of my non-mushing friends to the rundown of the race purse for an event like the Beargrease.

"You mean," they exclaim, "if you win, somebody just *hands* you a check for ten grand?"

To them, the figure seems completely out of proportion. After all, the race is run in just a few days. Within my circle of independent, liberal cohorts, the whole notion smacks of blatant greed and all-American wastefulness.

I remember being ecstatic when news of the first $50,000 purse for the Beargrease hit the local newspapers. A friend of mine, however, was worried by both the news and my response to it.

"I hope people won't start running it just for the money," she said gravely. I burst out laughing, which was evidently the wrong thing to do at the time.

There are two questions involved in a consideration of race winnings and the costs of fielding a team. First, are long-distance sled dog races of any value to anyone, to society, to "the world"? I would argue that they are. Such events draw people outdoors in winter, away from their television sets and video games, to witness a dramatic team effort by humans and animals. The races are colorful and exciting; they bring out the best in mushers, dogs, race workers and spectators.

Without races like the Iditarod, without events like the Boston Marathon or the Indianapolis 500 or the Kentucky Derby, would not the world be just a little drab, a little lacking in sparkle? Are we all here to simply do our duty, noses firmly pressed to the grindstone, pensions and dental-care benefits dangling before us like carrots? I think not. My dogs think not. They were born to run. And some mushers make it clear, by the success they achieve, that *they* were born to run them.

Secondly, if one can agree that a long-distance sled dog race is worthwhile (and not everyone can agree to this), then what should be the monetary gain that will allow the event to survive and the competitors to continue training and competing? What of purses like $10,000 for winning the Beargrease, $20,000 for the Yukon Quest and $50,000 for the Iditarod? They are not, I would argue, sums out of proportion to the years of effort and expense that go toward fielding a dogteam capable of winning these races. No musher who has ever seriously competed in such a race has any doubt that such earnings have indeed been *earned,* several times over.

So, in summer, between homestead projects and raising pups and jotting down notes on individual dogs, mushers raise money. We work, all of us, at some pursuit or profession that will bring in a predictable income. A few mushers can work within the field of dog mushing—building sleds, marketing feeds, raising and training and selling dogs—but most of us cannot. We are carpenters, or dentists, or lawyers, or salmon fishermen, or guides, or writers.

We seek sponsors. We write letters. We make phone calls. We assemble resumés of our experiences, photographs of our teams, records of our expenses. We search for the firm or institution or individual who can help us on our way, down the training trails to the starting line. Sometimes we succeed. Often we fail and continue on with a tightened budget and a thriftier outlook.

I recall the statement attributed to Libby Riddles in 1985 when she became the first woman musher to win the Iditarod and an overnight celebrity. She had no major corporate sponsor that year, although like many serious mushers she had made a determined effort to find one. "Thanks to all the people who *didn't* sponsor me," she said, "for keeping me tough!"

It is mid-August. A few leaves on the tiniest birch trees around the dog yard are turning yellow. At night it gets fully dark, for the first time in months. A newsletter arrived yesterday from the Beargrease Race and with it an entry form requiring a $500 payment. Banjo has had her pups, five females and a male. Elvis, born last December, is nearly full grown.

The supply of dog food from Ralston Purina Canada, one of our sponsors, has arrived by barge and is stacked in the shed—all 10,000 pounds of it.

The mornings are cool and getting cooler. Our first race of the coming season will start five months from today.

In the dog yard, Kodi lies on top of his house, opens one eye and yawns.

TOPKOK

JIM KERSHNER, ONE OF THE RACE JUDGES FOR THE 1987 Iditarod, had some mixed advice for me soon after I signed into the White Mountain checkpoint for our mandatory four-hour layover. The "official" advice was clear—all teams were to be strongly encouraged to remain in White Mountain. The weather was steadily worsening along the final 77 miles of the Iditarod Trail. The teams that had just finished, including veterans Herb Nayokpuk, Terry Adkins and Dee Dee Jonrowe, had faced white-out conditions along the entire final stretch of the trail beyond Topkok Head.

But Jim knew, from his own Iditarod racing, what it felt like to be in White Mountain with a dogteam and he knew that the best he could do for a tired, somewhat dazed group of mushers was to present the facts. Front Street and the huge wooden arch that marked the end of the Iditarod were just too close. The option of settling in at White Mountain, where the weather remained bright and mild, was just not going to find too many takers that afternoon. He knew this and so he drew me aside for some more in-depth, less "official" advice.

"You know it's going to be real bad around Topkok there. There's a stretch after you drop down off the bluff where it's just like a wind tunnel. The wind's out of the north and it screams right along the base of the mountains. But if you can get through there, maybe eight, ten miles, you might find it easing off just a little. If you've got a real good leader you might get through there. But it's going to be tough; I have to tell you not to go."

I nodded, hoping to seem fully coherent and capable of rationally considering my situation. But it was a bluff. It was 3 p.m. on Friday. In another two hours, we could be on the trail to Nome. The weather was good there in White Mountain, but the sky to the west, toward Topkok and the finish line, was washed out by the wispy haze that is the distant sign of an Arctic blizzard. I had heard of the Topkok "funnel" and its winds. Two nights before, I had spent 12 hours bivouacked in high winds near Lonely Hill, outside of Shaktoolik. That had not been any fun and what the race organization was trying to tell me was that the winds ahead were going to make that last blow seem like a stroll in the park.

It had been a disappointing race for us, that second run on the Iditarod Trail. I had come back to Alaska with high hopes, eager to set straight some of the many mistakes I had made as a rookie. I had a generous sponsor, the Safety-Kleen Corporation, and an improved team of dogs, including one that I had leased from defending champion Susan Butcher.

But it takes more than a year and a handful of good dogs to pay one's dues in the Iditarod Race. My team still lacked the consistency and depth of experience that are needed to compete seriously. I lacked the same—consistency and depth of experience.

Sickness had run rampant through most of the field of 62 dogteams over the first five days of the race. By Ophir, not even halfway to Nome, I had shipped out six of the dogs with whom I had begun the race. I still had the remaining nine and they would all be leaving White Mountain in harness.

We had fallen far off the pace; Susan had won the race on Wednesday, over 48 hours ago. We were in 28th place or thereabouts and there were four other teams clustered around us, all vying for a spot in the 20s: Kazuo Kojima, Bruce Barton, Gary Guy and Dan MacEachen. I felt eager for the race to be over; Kristen was waiting in Nome. I could always turn back if the conditions ahead proved impossible. So my deluded, fatigued train of thought went.

Gary Guy from Galena, Alaska, was there in White Mountain, facing the same advice and the same dilemma. I had grown to like him and appreciate his outlook during the past several days when our teams had been leapfrogging each other along the coast. He had a fast dogteam and was similarly disappointed with his standing in the race. He seemed particularly determined to keep track of me—evidently he wanted the final results to show clearly who had the better dogs. Yet along with his competitiveness I had sensed a maturity and level-headedness that I respect in any musher. He took good care of his dogs and did not let the selfish demands of pride and ego get in the way of sensible strategy.

We talked together as our teams slept side by side.

"I'm inclined to go. Just see how bad it really is," I began.

"Yeah," he answered, "but I'd feel awfully stupid pinned down out there when I could be here sitting in a hot tub."

Gary is a pilot, flying commercially for a small air service in Galena. Likewise, at that time, I made my living as a pilot in Ely, Minnesota. Perhaps, subconsciously, we were considering the forecast of bad weather as pilots instead of as dog mushers. In an airplane, even a small airplane, a common tactic is to simply fly close enough to bad weather to tell whether it truly lives up to its billing. If it does, one turns back and beats a hasty retreat into better conditions. If the weather seems less dismal than the forecast, one can fly on, ready at any time to execute that crucial 180-degree turn. In my addled late-Iditarod brain, I was adopting the same look-and-see approach to that coastal blizzard. In doing so, I was conveniently ignoring the fact that even a little Piper Cub flies ten times as fast as my dogteam would be moving during the coming night.

Slowly our plan evolved. We would hedge our bets by making a pact and facing the final stretch of trail as a pair of teams. We would not just travel together if it seemed convenient—we would leave White Mountain together, stop and start together and come either to Nome or the back side of the storm together. Two heads were better than one, we figured.

By 5 p.m. we were on the trail. My team pulled out of the checkpoint first, but Gary soon caught up with and passed us. We left the Nudyutok River almost immediately and began a slow steady climb through sparsely wooded hills. The wind from the northwest grew stronger with every mile. But visibility remained good and the anticipation of soon being in Nome was almost intoxicating.

Gary's team was definitely faster than mine. As we moved steadily west into the darkening evening and strong winds, he had to stop all too frequently to let my dogs close the gap between our teams. Such pauses are irritating to a driver and they quickly sap the momentum of a tired team. Finally, with an angry edge to his voice, Gary spoke up when we pulled in behind him.

"Listen. You're going to have to give those guys a kick in the ass. We've *got* to get over these hills and down out of here before it gets dark. If we don't, it's going to get dangerous."

"Yeah, O.K." I knew he was right. It was time to put the team into overdrive and the way I do that is with a few sharp cracks of a three-foot signal whip made of braided caribou hide. I rummaged in the back pouch of my sled bag and pulled out the whip, which I had not touched in the 1,000 miles since we'd left Anchorage.

My whip is something that, as a serious dog trainer, I do not use without considerable forethought. For the dogs who have tasted its sting, in reprimand for a serious fight or some other major transgression, the sight of the whip and the sound of its crack are enough to touch off a flood of adrenalin and a wild rush forward powered by sheer panic. Even dogs that have never felt the lash seem to assimilate the tremendous respect and fear that their partners have for it.

I kicked my snowhook into the hard-packed crust and walked up alongside the team. I was talking tough: "All right, let's get up there, Tex! D. J.! Morris! Getup! Banjo!" There was a rough growl in my voice and I was swinging the whip back and forth menacingly.

Every few seconds I gave it a sharp pop in the air. It was time to rely on this primal message in order to accomplish the task at hand. My tired dogs had no way to conceive of the storm that lay ahead, or of the danger of being caught up in those hills by it. I simply had to speed them up.

When I pulled the hook once again I could tell that we were definitely in high gear. Maxima and D. J., the two young wheel dogs, dug in with a savage burst of power. We flew along the trail until my leaders, Beaver and Morris, were ready to climb onto Gary's sled. He turned to me and grinned and made a quick thumb-up signal with his mitt. We would stay together now, with no waiting or delay.

The daylight was fading; it was nearly 8:30 p.m. We passed a tiny A-frame shelter cabin at a small creek and sidehilled away from it toward the prominent seaside bluff called Topkok Head. The storm was just ahead of us. The sky to the west was dim and the horizon was indistinguishable. As we climbed and descended several long hills, I remembered my last day on the race the year before, when we had passed through those hills just at dawn on Sunday morning. It was Friday night now, I mused, so we *were* running a faster race this year. Unfortunately, so was almost everyone else. With any luck, we'd shave at least 34 hours from our 1986 time. I was still planning on getting to Nome by morning.

It was not until we had begun the descent of Topkok's west side that we paused for a decent rest break. It was fully dark by then. As we clung to the edge of the steep trail, we adjusted our headlamps, sipped from our juice bottles and gave snacks of fish and meat to our dogs. After about 30 minutes, we continued down into the wind tunnel at the base of Topkok. The rest of the night became a blur.

Imagine running a dogteam on the wing of a jet that is flying through a snowstorm. Such was the feeling I had for the next several hours as we encountered the full fury of that storm. In the darkness the dogs were being tossed *sideways* through the air, picked up in pairs and set down again four feet to the south. We ran our two teams in a single line, changing off in lead several times, with the rear team's leaders almost between the legs of the front musher. When we stopped the dogs and tried to move toward each other to talk, we staggered and lurched with movements that would have been hilarious if they had not been fundamentally frightening. I had never felt such wind. And Gary, from Galena on the Yukon River, was likewise a newcomer to the severity of a Bering Sea blizzard. We were the blind leading the blind and our dogs were easily the most levelheaded members of our group as we struggled aimlessly at the foot of Topkok Head.

And through it all, amazingly, I was *falling asleep!* Such is the special curse of the Iditarod musher—I was out with a team of dogs in nerve-wracking conditions that demanded common sense and good judgment and at the same time I was nearly delirious from exertion and lack of sleep. Several times, after we had made the belated decision to attempt a retreat, I found myself dozing off.

I woke to watch strange hallucinations move through the midst of that bizarre montage: blowing dogs and the crouched figure of Gary were joined in the beam of my headlamp by nonexistent trees, huge boulders and several late-model cars.

Finally, after several emphatic disagreements, mainly because I wanted to continue west based on what Jim Kershner had told me—though I doubt now that there would have been any improvement in that direction—we did the only thing we could do: we stopped.

None of our instincts learned from past seasons of bush and tundra travel with the dogs could come into play that night. In a storm, in the north, one makes camp. Tent, stove and a picket line for the dogs are set up. The object of the game is simply to dig in, get comfortable and wait it out. But our sleds that night were stripped bare for the final dash to Nome. After hearing the forecast we had left nothing behind in White Mountain, but we had both jettisoned gear in checkpoints farther back along the trail. Gary had even changed sleds and was driving a short, light "finishing sled" that was just the ticket for a final jaunt to Nome. However, its sled bag was tiny and there was no way he could have adopted the musher's last resort in a storm—to climb into the sled, pull tight the cover and wait in relative comfort until conditions improved.

Luckily, it was not bitterly cold. I do not think the temperature dropped below zero at any time during the storm. With Gary's sled unusable as shelter, I could not in good conscience bid him "good evening" and crawl into my own spacious sled bag. And my sled, though spacious, was not big enough for two. We managed to zip our sleeping bags together and make a very drafty, uncomfortable double bivouac under the leeward side of my tipped-over sled. Our dogs were all unhooked from their tuglines and they quickly piled themselves into a pair of snow-covered heaps.

It was a long night. The wind increased until I thought sure we would be plucked off the ground and tossed into the ocean somewhere nearby to the south. The air was completely filled with spindrift. Visibility was in the range of four to eight feet. I learned later that the winds in Nome that night were clocked at about 100 miles per hour.

I was not concerned, in those first few hours, as I dozed and shifted in the awkward space beneath the sled. I had been in storms before, many times, though never had I faced one of such intensity with such minimal gear. It couldn't blow forever, I thought to myself. Gary seemed worried, though, and he was colder than I was. I knew I needed to remain stoic and cheerful.

"And to think I could be sitting in White Mountain, having a nice big hamburger and soaking in a hot tub," I mumbled. A sullen "yep" was my partner's only response.

Above the barren strip of gravel beach the wind-driven snow gradually brightened with the coming of dawn. The wind seemed to be blowing as hard as it had been all night. Gary was awake when I stirred, mumbled and struggled in the cramped, wet sleeping bag.

"We have to get sorted out here," he said seriously. "This is bad news. Everything's full of snow. And wet."

I scrunched my hat up off my forehead and looked around. He was right. Our entire world was a white fog. Everything we had was either coated with snow, completely buried, or damp where the spindrift had melted onto it. The air was semi-solid: if a bare hand was exposed for just a moment it turned instantly wet from the melting of tiny crystals on warm skin.

All that day we struggled in a losing battle against the creeping cold and dampness. With a snow shovel we carved out a low cave and with some poles that we miraculously found just ten feet from our "camp" we rigged a makeshift roof of snowblocks and sleds.

In the afternoon we roused and fed our teams some meat from our scant supplies. The dogs seemed completely content; they were faring far better than we were. The process of starting Gary's stove and melting some snow for water took over two hours, with the spindrift filling every nook and cranny of the apparatus.

In fact, our snow-hole was a miserable excuse for a shelter and it could well have been a death trap if the storm had been colder and had prevailed for several more days. There was simply no escaping the nearly microscopic crystals of wind-driven snow. We were damp, tired, dehydrated and hungry. I realized, for the first time in my life, that hypothermia does not strike only weekend campers in bluejeans and polo shirts. If something did not change here within 24 to 36 hours, I thought, we were going to be in big trouble.

Several times that day we heard the distant drone of aircraft. We knew there would be some concern for us in Nome and probably some race officials were already upset by our blatant disregard for their advice. Our job, at that point, was simple—to weather the storm, care for the dogs and get to Nome. If we could do that, we would probably not face too much wrath upon our arrival.

That evening we thought we detected a subtle shift in the wind, backing slightly into the west. We talked of moving on, but decided we needed a more consistent improvement in order to leave even the meager protection of our camp. By six p.m. we had climbed into our sleeping bags in the small hollow of our shelter. We lay there, listening to the rush of the wind. Gary smoked his last cigarette and shared a few puffs of it with me. I felt relaxed again and confident that by morning we would be able to move. But my companion seemed wetter and colder and less hopeful than I was.

After only an hour, Gary got up to answer the call of nature—not a pleasant task in such conditions. As he struggled upward out of our cave, I heard him exclaim, "Hey, it's breaking."

"Huh?" I murmured, half awake.

"It's breaking up. I can see part way down the shore. And the wind's down a little."

"Yeah, I think we'll be out of here come morning."

"Morning, hell. We can be out of here right *now*. You game?"

That remark got me up and instantly alert. This guy is talking about leaving for Nome, I thought, just because he can see 20 feet!

"No, really," he continued, "I think we should hit it. We can travel in this stuff. It'll only get better to the west."

I was not convinced. I climbed out and pulled on my wind parka. Our bleak world was suddenly a little larger—piled-up dogs, gravel beach, glare ice on a small lagoon, a few blades of grass. The wind *had* gone down a bit.

Suddenly, I was heartily sick of damp, filthy clothing, cramped quarters and uncertainty. To move west was to guarantee only one thing—we would not spend another night *here*. And that seemed to be enticing enough to both of us.

"Well, yeah, I guess I'm game."

In about 40 minutes we were underway. There was nothing to pack up at that campsite. The most striking aspect of the whole chore was its simplicity. There were the dogs, the sleds, our clothes and sleeping bags and that was all. The storm had robbed us of only one thing. One of my snowshoes had been blown away during the night, from alongside the sled. I had never before experienced a wind capable of picking up and carrying something as awkward as a snowshoe. I had set it down for a moment and it was instantly tumbling south toward the open ocean. Maybe someday it will wash up on the beach at Waikiki.

We were back in formation, one team's leaders tucked beside the leading team's sled. The storm was abating, but it was still ferocious. Dogs were still being buffeted sideways along the trail, but now we could see ahead beyond our lead dogs. We were able to keep to the trail along the coast, which was marked by large wooden tripods. By 9 p.m. the brief respite in the storm seemed to be ending, though, and it was getting dark. As I began to ponder the grim scenario of pitching another miserable camp, a miraculous vision appeared off to our right. It was a cabin—a tiny yellow cabin.

We were home free. We holed up that night in that little cabin on the beach and read the stories penciled on its walls of other Iditarod and Alaska Sweepstakes teams that had taken refuge there over the years. We added our names and a terse summary of our . . . our what? Adventure? Ordeal? Mistake? Somehow none of those words seem to match the experience, though there were elements of all three.

We thawed the last of our combined dog rations to make a watery gruel for our teams and we stoked the woodstove all evening in a frantic effort to dry our gear. That night I suffered the only frostbite of the storm when, while I rummaged in my sled, the blast of the wind found the space between my glove and the cuff of my coverall sleeve. A long thin blister formed there and stayed as a reminder of that hellacious wind.

The next morning, the storm was past. The wind still blew strongly from the northwest, but visibility was good and the clouds had lifted. Most importantly, the blowing snow and ground drift had ceased. I suddenly realized that, after all we had been through, Gary was still racing me to Nome. As I poured a cup of coffee and settled back into my chair in the small hut, he eyed me with a look that seemed to say, "Relax in Nome, not here." I jumped up and swigged the hot coffee, acting as if I hadn't *really* intended to take my time. He smiled.

There had been other teams stranded in the storm. Through the worst of it, we had wondered how they were faring. As we moved down the coast toward Safety roadhouse, we came upon a dismal sight. A quarter mile south of the trail sat a sled and with it an indistinct pile of snow-covered lumps that could have been a dogteam. I steered my team toward it and as we approached I began to worry. There was no movement in the sled when I called "whoa" to my dogs. I walked up to the sled bag half expecting to find a frozen musher inside. Gary pulled up and walked over.

"Hey Bruce! Wake up!" he yelled. It was Bruce Barton's sled and in a second there emerged from the cover of the sled bag the most bedraggled, snow-encrusted dog puncher I have ever seen. It was Bruce, dazed and slightly incoherent. He had been in that sled, sealed off totally from the outside world, for 40 hours straight.

We lingered long enough there to help him hook up his team and start moving and he followed behind us as we headed for Safety. Never has that odd checkpoint name seemed more appropriate. As we paused there and recounted our story of the storm, we learned that Kazuo Kojima and Dan MacEachen had also been unaccounted for over the past two nights. Both emerged from their hideouts later that morning.

It is 22 miles from Safety to the finish line in Nome. "You've been a hell of a nice guy through all this," said Gary, "but I really don't think I should let you beat me, you know?"

"Let's race then," I grinned. "Get those mangy hounds of yours out of here or it'll be too late." But I knew my response was pure jest. Gary's team was superior to mine; they had shown that throughout the race. The only reason we had come this far together was by virtue of some tortoise-and-hare maneuvering on my part.

Three hours later, 11 minutes behind Gary, we crossed the finish line on Front Street. The crowd there was large, since we were the first two teams to arrive in

Nome for over 36 hours. We were warmly greeted by everyone and the dogs rested that night on thick straw in the huge dog lot along Nome's waterfront. There was no chastisement for our decision to leave White Mountain. We had paid for that decision already.

As the Federal Aviation Administration tells pilots, "Good judgment comes from experience. Experience comes from poor judgment."

FOR TWO OLD
FRIENDS

I HAVE OWNED WELL OVER 100 DIFFERENT DOGS DURING
my relatively short career as a musher. Some of my
friends and acquaintances in the sled dog world own that
many or more at any given time, so the number 100 is
not remarkable in itself. But it is a large number, especially when one is referring to dogs, since in their lifetimes most people come to know only four or five dogs
at most.

I have kept these many dogs at all different stages
of life. I have known some of them from the moment
of their birth to the moment of their death. For a few
of them, it was I who arranged conception and I who,
many years later, arranged the means and accepted the
timeliness of death.

Which one of these dogs was the best? That is a
silly and impossible question, really. Many among them
have been, at different times, both the best and the worst
dogs I have ever owned. Perhaps there is a young dog
out in my yard as I write, growing and maturing to become the best dog—the toughest, smartest, fastest dog—
with whom I have ever worked.

Two of the dogs whose distinctive natures I will always treasure are gone. Their names were Popcorn and Morris and they both came into my life as full-grown, middle-aged dogs. They each taught me more in our time together than I ever taught either of them. Rarely do I run a team of dogs without thinking, at least briefly, of one of them. They were both males, Popcorn a wheel dog and Morris a leader.

Popcorn came to me as a part of my first dogteam. In fact, as the father of every dog in it. Although dates and details are somewhat sketchy, he came originally from the dogs of Jerry Riley, a Nenana, Alaska, musher with a long record of tough, hard-driven teams that can be traced back to the "old-time" Alaska breeds. Somehow, Popcorn came as a pup to a racing kennel in Minnesota, but it was soon clear that he was not built for a career as a speedster. Duncan Storlie purchased him for use on Lynx Track courses. He almost failed there, too, since in those first few seasons "Popper" was so flighty and tense that he quivered to the touch.

Popcorn matured to become a wheel dog of the old school. He had a long, low physique and his entire musculature seemed to be formed of tempered steel. Over those wiry muscles was a scrawny black and white coat of short coarse hair. He had a broad, wolfish skull with a long muzzle reminiscent of a collie. His tail was long and ratty, with a distinctive crook in its white tip. He was, on his best days, "striking." On other days, when he had just crawled out of a deeply melted snow hole after a night of −40-degree weather, he was downright ugly.

Through all the time I knew him, we who fed him had a constant struggle to keep his weight up. With his thin fur and turbocharged metabolism, he would sink into the snow like a hot stone with every passing minute of rest along the trail. He was the first dog I knew for whom a wool overcoat was standard camp apparel. In his prime, hardened by a season of good food and hard work, he weighed over 85 pounds. Even at that weight his pelvis and backbone were knobby and he looked like the epitome of the long-suffering beast of burden.

Some huskies are fighters and some, like Popcorn, are lovers. Though capable of defending himself and teaching a quick, painful lesson to any dog that challenged him, he always seemed to do so with a somewhat bored attitude. His passion was *passion*. Over the years he became the cornerstone of the sled dog breeding that Duncan and Will were doing and thereby also the father or grandfather or great-grandfather of many of Steger's now-famous dogs: Soapy, Zap, Chester and Gordy. Season after season he was bred to two Siberian husky sisters, Bluebelle and Blossom, who came originally from the kennel of Tim White.

This constant reinforcement of his procreative urge served only to make him, by the end of his life, an incurable old sex maniac. If there was a female in season within 50 miles of his doghouse, Popcorn seemed capable of sensing her by some supernatural power and he would spend hours and days and *weeks* alternately crooning atop his house and lunging against his stake-out chain, moaning pitiably. His groveling, slobbering eagerness was an embarrassment to his gender.

But Popper had one other all-consuming desire in life: work. Hard, low-down, wheel-dog work, in small teams on unbroken trails, with novice mushers and tenfoot sleds full of firewood, were his calling in life. To watch Popcorn working in wheel on a narrow, twisted trail, lunging and bracing and popping his tugline at all the right moments, was like watching a virtuoso in concert. His movements and timing were perfect. He was the epitome of sled-dog aptitude and experience.

Popcorn would never have made the grade on a long-distance racing team. His top cruising speed was probably about eight miles per hour and his all-out sprints probably did not carry him over 12 miles per hour for very long. Fortunately, I had a chance to work with him and learn from him at a time when such parameters were of no importance to me.

It would be impossible to prove, but I think Popcorn may have saved a person's life more than once. I know that he certainly saved me and others at various times from some miserable and dangerous situations. One such event occurred during a long trip on the Canadian barrenlands in 1981. The third member of our three-man, ten-dog expedition, John Mordhorst, had been flown out when his mother suffered a stroke. Kurt Mitchell and I were traveling west again with a gigantic load that still makes me shake my head when I recall it. Popcorn was in wheel, along with his son Sinker, one evening as we climbed west out of the Hanbury-Thelon river basin.

My journal tells the story: "... I got the dogs moving again, only to see that Kurt had disappeared over a slight rise. The hilltop was blown nearly clean, exposing sharp rocks that tore into the bottom of the sled. Suddenly, one huge chunk of jagged stone stopped us completely. I lunged again and again, screaming my shouts of encouragement to the dogs. Finally the sled budged, with superdog effort from Popcorn, and we moved ahead over the knoll. It was clear that we had lost the trail and at that moment the left runner rode up on a boulder and the top-heavy load tipped completely over.

"It must have been quite a scene, but there was no other person there to watch it. I cursed at the top of my lungs and the dogs promptly sat down, evidently fed up with the onslaughts of my temper. Kurt was just a dim silhouette in the twilight and then he was gone completely again. The wind, the wind, the wind.

"I stumbled ahead, nearly blinded by rage and the clammy frozen mucus-and-foam shell of my face mask, sinking to my thighs in soft drifts. I knew the trail was off to the left somewhere, but it wouldn't do to have the dogs turn while the sled was still on its side. I tried to break a trail ahead and soon fell completely over, thrashing my fists on the snow in helpless anger. I laid there a moment and suddenly fear hit me. It was nearly dark. Blowing snow. Kurt somewhere out ahead, with no insulation

save the sweat-dampened clothes on his back. The dogs digging
in, the sled overturned, the trail somewhere to the south. That
fear gripped me for a moment and delivered its ultimatum: Get
up and get moving, calm down and find Kurt's trail, or face
the consequences.

"I marched back to the sled, crouched beside it, braced a
shoulder under the stanchion and called to the dogs. Popcorn
rose to his feet and the others followed his example. It was
uncanny; some strange new communication seemed to flow between us. With a shout, I heaved against the sled and Popcorn
hit his tug about five times within two seconds. The sled began
to move, across the last of the stones and into the deep drifts.
Desperate to keep it moving, I shouted to the dogs. Floundering
in the snow, the leaders moved off to the left, toward the trail.
Popcorn and Sinker kept up their insane jackhammer tugs on
the bridle and the huge sled's momentum was maintained. By
luck, I shouted 'Gee' just as Turok and Mukluk reached the
wind-scoured trace that was the trail. We moved ahead, angling
down the slope into that beautiful little clump of stunted spruce.
'Let's go home, doggers! Popper, when we get home I'm gonna
buy you two tons of ground round and tie you up with Bluebelle
for a year!' "

That night and many other nights, at the end of
long, cold, tiring days, Popcorn's indomitable strength
and spirit made a crucial difference. It is easy to sing the
praises of a dog whose working days are over; no one
can ever again test the accuracy of the claims I make for
Popcorn. But many mushers have known a dog like him
and those special dogs are part of what make mushing
so worthwhile and so hopelessly addicting. No Yamaha
or Ski-Doo, no Polaris or ATV ever won the heart of its
owner the way a dog like Popcorn did.

As Popcorn aged, he began to lose some of his
strength and speed. This change in him coincided with
the seasons when I was beginning to concentrate more
on the overall speed of my team and to have aspirations
as a long-distance racer. Popcorn was big, too big, and
he was 12 years old at the start of the 1984 training

season. He joined the group of freighting dogs that I leased to the Voyageur Outward Bound school. For this work he would have been perfectly suited in his prime. But he was past his prime.

As the training of the school's dogs progressed under the guidance of Catie Maloney, it became clear to both of us that Popcorn's working days were over. He had stiffened badly in the hindquarters and could not begin to match even the slow pace set by his teammates. Furthermore, it began to look as though he was in nearly constant pain. His gait was halting and on some mornings he seemed to be so stiff and sore that I wondered if he would ever get up again.

When the rest of the dogs were loaded into the truck for a trip or hooked up on the edge of the yard for a run, Popcorn would bark and bawl incessantly. He wanted desperately to join them. His mind was still willing and eager, but his body was not.

One day at the height of the winter's busiest period, when I was nearly alone at the school, I walked to the dog yard. As I approached, Popcorn emerged from his house and looked directly at me. We held each other's gaze for many minutes. He was the only dog in the yard. The sleds were gone, the teams were spread far and wide in campsites and along the trails of the border country. Only old Popper was left and as he hobbled across his circle, looking intently at me, I knew it was time.

He had asked me, in his way, to do what I knew I must do. The scientists will scoff at such blatant anthropomorphism. I might too, if he had been any other dog. But with Popcorn I had left behind the objective outlook of the modern animal trainer. He had me by the heart.

I walked to my little house-trailer and got my rifle. With heavy, slow steps I went back up the hill to the dog yard. Popcorn still sat there and his gaze still said the same thing to me.

We walked together far out past the last of the school's buildings, roads and paths, into a thick patch of second-growth poplar near the Kawishiwi River. I said some small, serious things to Popcorn and I patted those bony shoulders of his one last time. The sound of a shot cracked through the cold air and it was over. Hard-nosed dog musher that I was, I had to hide out in my trailer for several hours before the redness and tears left my eyes.

Morris was, in many ways, the exact opposite of Popcorn. He was a handsome dog, jet black with pure white stockings, light on his feet and with a certain unmistakable classiness in his bearing. Morris did not just trot—he had a flashy, high-stepping gait like that of a hackney horse. Morris did not just *respond* to gee and haw commands—he did so with a flourish and sharpness all his own. While Popcorn seemed completely absorbed in the concerns of his life as a dog, I always had the feeling that Morris secretly aspired to be human.

Morris came from Alaska and to my team after a succession of owners in northern Minnesota. Evidently, Gary Hokkanen brought him south and Morris ran in the team that Gary drove to victory in the original version of the Beargrease Race. From that team, Morris went to musher Chris Lange of Buyck, Minnesota. From there to a recreational musher in Ely and on to my friend Kevin Molloy. Whether by virtue of his gradual change with age, or by a different set of standards on Kevin's part, Morris finally blossomed and was appreciated as a member of that seven-dog team.

Much reference is made to lead dogs wherever dog mushing is discussed. One often encounters mushers who seem to be constantly shopping for "a good leader." Nowhere in the realm of dog mushing are there more intangibles and variables than in the relationships of mushers and lead dogs. Kevin's work with Morris was an inspiring example of the fact that necessity is the best producer of lead dogs that there has ever been. The *need* for a dependable leader and the determination and patience to train one bear results far more lasting and satisfying than expensive attempts to *buy* such a dog.

Here I refer to working lead dogs—"blue-collar leaders." Such dogs might go the distance in the Iditarod and they might cruise at 12 miles an hour when everything is just right, but when there are sawlogs to be hauled from a thicket half a mile from a good trail, or progress to be made over glare ice or through a whiteout, or when the sled is drastically overloaded, they still get the job done. Morris, despite his inauspicious early years, became such a leader as he grew older.

Like the young Popcorn, the young Morris was, by all accounts, a basket case. He was insanely eager, with none of the temperance or patience that maturity brings. He would charge ahead with all-out abandon until his energy was used up. Then he would abruptly quit and literally drop in the traces. One season it seemed to have become a hopelessly ingrained habit with him, according to Chris Lange. He would reach a certain spot along a certain training trail and down he would go. It is not surprising that he changed owners so many times. He was lucky that there were always other mushers willing to give him a try.

At the age of six, Morris began to settle down. Though still a frothing, babbling idiot during the moments when the team was being harnessed, he became capable of putting in a full day's work. Gradually, his intelligence and tractability shone through his wild-eyed fervor. Under Kevin's guidance, over months of cross-country travel on large trailless lakes, Morris became an open country gee-haw leader. That long phrase translates as a dog capable of being steered solely by voice commands across a wide expanse of sea ice, tundra, or snow-covered lake.

Once a musher has had the pleasure of driving such a lead dog, he or she is spoiled for life. With every subtle inflection of the musher's voice, there is a predictable adjustment of the team's heading. With Morris, Mukluk, McDougal, Beaver and Banjo—the five good leaders I have run in ten years of mushing—there is usually no need to shout. In fact, on a still, −40-degree morning, it is possible to *whisper* the commands from the back of the sled.

Running a newly trained leader in unfamiliar tree-less country, map in hand, steering by compass and by voice commands, is a thrill that must be akin to riding a young horse flawlessly through its paces in an equestrian event. There is at such moments the realization that the animals are making exhilarating something that would be tedious or impossible without their cooperation.

Luckily for me, Morris changed owners one final time in 1985, when Kevin traded him to me as part of a complex deal involving two old pickup trucks and half a dozen dogs. At first, I was leery of Kevin's claims for this odd black dog with the hackney gait. After all, I thought, if he was so great why was he running for his fifth musher in five years?

Gradually, though, "Maurice" won me over. Kevin had coined the nickname Morris the Clown for him and as I grew to understand him it seemed to fit. He was the only dog I have met who would willingly pose in sunglasses and a baseball cap for long enough to get his portrait snapped. With his flop ear where cartilage had been torn in a fight, his squarish snout and steep forehead, he was always the topic of a few remarks whenever a visitor came to the dog yard.

On the Churchill River, when Mike and I would let a dog or two into our cabin for an evening visit and a warm nap, we always looked forward to the arrival of Morris. While some dogs looked thoroughly miserable during their entire stay indoors and cowered in whatever dark corner they could find, Morris would stride confidently through the doorway and glance from side to side as if he was the chairman of a huge corporation just arriving at a board meeting. Then he would invariably lift his leg on all four posts of the wooden table and prance over to each of us for some petting and friendly ridicule.

As a racer, Morris was only a partial success. He never completed a run in the Beargrease, except for that run as a yearling in Gary Hokkanen's team. He was plagued by the nagging shoulder injuries that are especially common on the short steep hills of the North Shore Trail. But he twice finished the Iditarod and led us through the Topkok blizzard, the snowless Burn and all the other demanding tests of a rookie and second-year team.

For two years straight, wherever and whenever I hooked up dogs, Morris was the first to be put in harness and the last to be taken out again. He was not fast, but he did have the odd knack of *appearing* to fly down the trail, his white wrists flashing, when in fact he was poking along at a dismal eight miles an hour. In lead, he was thus more important as a navigator than as a pacesetter and I tried to run him always with a faster partner.

I left ten of my dogs with a friend in Fort Resolution, on the south shore of Great Slave Lake, on our way home from Alaska in 1987. Within several months, I was to be returning to Canada as an immigrant and moving directly out to the Hoarfrost River. It seemed more sensible to leave my dogs up north and spare them the long trip back and forth across the prairies in the heat of summer.

The dogs fared well that spring and when I landed my little Cub floatplane in Mission Bay just west of Fort Resolution in early July, I was eager to see them again. They looked good—healthy and well fed. But four days before my arrival, while I was flying slowly north from Ely to Great Slave Lake, Morris had become suddenly, violently ill. His body had been wracked by horrible convulsions and his breathing had been desperate and gasping. The nurse and the many experienced mushers in town had done their best to save him, but after three days of ceaseless suffering my friend Ted had seen enough. In the hot dry dust of the dog yard outside Fort Resolution, Morris' wandering journey ended.

I have a yearling sired by Morris named McLeod and already I see some of his father coming out in him. He is jet black with white socks and he has a confidence and a panache that threaten my objectivity. In the winters ahead, perhaps he can fill his old man's dog booties. But it won't be easy.

Popcorn and Morris were memorable dogs. As I write of them I realize that one value in doing so is that they become representatives for thousands of sled dogs and for the relationships that countless mushers have with their teams. Anecdotes and anthropomorphism—dog stories—are at the heart of the spirit of mushing. We see facets of ourselves in every dog with whom we work closely. We ultimately see sled dogs not simply as programmed, mindless automatons, but as individuals.

Not all dogs become more attractive and responsive to us over time. Some are dogs' dogs and give the clear message that for humanity they do not give a hoot. But most of my dogs are my good friends. For a few rare ones like Popcorn and Morris, I have a respect and appreciation that goes even beyond friendship and becomes love.

SPRING TRAINING

FOR TWO DAYS NOW I HAVE BEEN PACKED AND READY. It is Friday morning, April 15. With my first glance out the cabin window at the thermometer, the tattered flag that serves as my windsock and the distant southern and eastern horizons it is obvious that this will be the day. It is −20 degrees, dead calm and the visibility is limitless.

On Wednesday, the day I had planned to depart, the temperature had risen above 45 degrees for the first time in six months. With a long climb toward the barrenlands awaiting the dogs and me, I had held off. That evening a brisk spring snowstorm had blown in, reducing visibility to less than 100 yards for the fifth time in two weeks. All the next day the storm had raged; travel on familiar territory would by no means have been impossible, but it would not have been pleasant. And I am determined that this trip is going to be, above all, pleasant.

The racing season is over and the disciplined regimen of a dogteam in training—precise mileages, exacting diet and feeding times, all of the tight routine that goes into preparation for competition—has fallen slack. I drink

209

my morning coffee and eat breakfast, do the usual chores around the homestead. I make a few final changes in the sled load, leaving behind some food, mainly, since we would now be out only three days instead of five. I heat a kettle of water so that I can carry tea and a bottle of juice in the sled.

I wonder about whether or not to carry my rifle. All winter it has ridden in the sled, as much out of consent to local custom as anything. But there are moose in the country that might not relinquish a hard-packed trail if surprised by a team of dogs in this season of deep soft snow. That somewhat flimsy argument for carrying a gun is backed up by the ever-present chance of another spring storm, a delay and slim rations for the dogs over a long homeward trail. There are caribou moving through the area, not many right now, but enough that the rifle stays in the load. It is six pounds of insurance and, perhaps, romanticism, in a stained and frayed canvas scabbard.

The sled is loaded. My nerves are on edge now. This setting off alone with my dogs into country partly familiar and partly new to me is an endeavor I do not take lightly. So much can happen out there. The dogs and I will be alone on the tundra. "Lose your team, lose your life," the adage tossed around by the old barrenland trappers, goes through my thoughts. Well, maybe not your *life,* in mid-April, I think. But still, the possibility of a lost team looms large in my all-too-vivid imagination.

I tow the sled to the spot alongside the dog yard where the trail out onto the ice begins. It is the sled I used in the Iditarod last year, resplendent with its bright blue sled bag catching the spring sunlight. But while I tow it and my glance goes over it, I notice that an important small bolt at the front end has been forced upward through the polyethylene bed of the toboggan. I find the tools needed to make a workable repair. Another ten minutes slide past. It's going to be nearly noon before we get out of here, I mutter.

I think now about the dogs. Twelve names are on the scribbled list that hangs from a nearby spruce tree. Twelve dogs will give me a lot of power, much more than I need in the early part of the day. Fresh and with a couple of days of rest behind them, they will have no shortage of the drive and wild-hearted "attitude" that all mushers so admire and that occasionally causes us such trouble. I wonder about being out on the lakes and barrens with that many, especially alone, especially early in the day when they are most enthusiastic. Nightmarish scenarios begin to crowd into my mind. For a moment I stand still.

On the spruce tree hitching post, a piece of cardboard is impaled on a nail just beneath my list of dogs. It was torn from a box containing produce and the words "Keep Cool" are printed on it in neat red letters. I stuck it there as a reminder to myself, back in January. Yeah, I tell myself now, just keep cool.

I stretch out the long gangline, with positions for seven pairs of dogs. This extra space gives me flexibility to shift from two leaders to a single leader and to run any of the team dogs without a partner. I anchor the sled to the cutoff spruce, secure each harness to a tugline with a carved hardwood toggle and walk over to get McDougal. The dog yard comes alive. Suddenly everyone is screaming and bawling their various reasons for coming along today, for being hooked up next and for not liking their neighbor. The result is nearly deafening.

McDougal is in harness and next to him is Beaver. Old reliable Beaver, who has been having a spotty year in training and racing, but upon whom I still rely when I need honesty out in front. I scamper back and forth, uphill to get a new dog, down to the gangline with the candidate lunging and wheeling and hopping along. Gradually the team takes shape and my pace quickens. With all 12 dogs in place I make a hasty final check as the dogs whine and scream and bark, frantically dig holes in the snow—anything to start burning some of that seemingly boundless energy. Maps. Sun goggles. Mitts. A mental check that the stove in the cabin is damped. With a foot on the brake and a hand on the snowhook, I shout to the leaders and lift the hook off the stump when a brief bit of slack comes into the line.

It's always the same. It's always fast and crazy and the air suddenly feels 30 degrees cooler as I straighten up on the runners and move swiftly out onto the lake. No worries about a trail for this section, at least—even after the storm yesterday, the tracks from my neighbors' visit of three days before are etched deeply into the springtime crust of snow, leading straight south 11 miles to Reliance.

The team is strung out ahead, each dog in its place, untangled and running hard. I ride the brake lightly now and look to be sure that my wrist is still held to the handlebar by the little loop of quarter-inch line. We are away, free and easy. I reach for my parka and glance at my watch. It's 11:45. Damn, but it takes a long time to get going some days.

Ten minutes out from the Hoarfrost River, the team begins to settle one by one into a steady fast trot. "Good dogs, you guys are good dogs," I tell them. Gone for us all today is the pressure of competition, the urge to constantly push the limit, perform with the utmost efficiency, get from the team all it can give. The air is like a refreshing cool drink as I suck in a deep breath. All I can hear is the soft, steady panting of a dozen dogs and the skidding of sled runners on snow crust.

Although it is not the most direct route to Pike's Portage, I have steered toward Reliance to take advantage of this trail and to avoid the tiring process of driving an eager team through a 15-mile stretch of untracked, crusted snow. This way is four miles longer but much faster, all in all.

At 12:45 we round Fairchild Point and swing in beneath my neighbors' cabin, which sits high on a granite promontory. Soon Roger and Bruce appear on the hill, preceded by little Dumoresq, two years old, who comes toward us, half-sliding, half-running, to greet some of his friends in the team. I kneel to pound the snowhook firmly into the ice, give my dogs a wary glance and walk over to say hello. I am not too keen on the prospect of leaving the team unattended so early in the day.

The three of us exchange greetings and small talk for a few moments. There had been an airplane in Reliance earlier that day, bringing mail and supplies for the government's weather station. Bruce asks if I would like to see my mail.

"No," I tell him, "I'll get it later; I'm on vacation now." I tell them my plans, to go to Artillery Lake and into the barrens from there, to be back in a couple of days. They wish me good luck, the dogs begin to yap and whine and I step back onto the sled.

I lift the snowhook and we bolt across Police Bay, straight for the weather station. I try in vain to steer McDougal and Beaver from the enticing prospect of a reunion with a couple of loose dogs at the station and finally resort to tipping the sled over, walking up and hauling them "Gee!" by the neckline. With several wistful glances over their shoulders, they round the point and we leave Reliance behind. Six miles to the start of Pike's Portage—actually a 25-mile series of trails and small lakes—the ancient route to Artillery Lake and the barrenlands.

The trail is hard and smooth. Just four days ago, the local trappers all pulled their final loads in from their camps on the barrens, behind four separate snow machines. This has left a perfect trail unaffected by yesterday's blowing snow, at least here on the open lake.

I muse over my brief stop as I move back into solitude. Talk has already turned to spring, to a planned May outing to an open creek south of Reliance, a few days of camping there—eating fish, trading stories and basking in sunshine on a bugless sand beach. It all seems a long way off today as we approach the start of the climb toward the tundra and pass a long-abandoned toboggan drifted in alongside the trail. I snug up the parka ruff around my neck.

Ahead on the ice are some dark specks. If I intently try to make them look like bedded caribou, I can. I am expert at creating such illusions for myself—pressure ridges become long lines of caribou, scrub trees become wolverines, boulders become wolves. But this is no illusion, for one of the specks has just risen and is now watching us approach. The dogs are, so far, oblivious to them. There is no wind. We move closer—more specks rise and suddenly McDougal has them in sight. I feel the surge of the handlebar in my grip as the dogs suddenly shift from a trot to a full-out gallop.

"Caribou!" I shout. Next year that will be my "get up" word for the team, I've decided.

It is impossible to describe adequately the burst of energy and acceleration that a team makes when on the trail of a band of caribou. Perhaps a fighter pilot would understand it. Were it possible to call it up at will, the musher would possess a truly magical power. Nothing, no trained response whether positively or negatively reinforced, can match the genuine enthusiasm of a team on the chase. I do not attempt to curb the dogs, so long as they stay on the trail. The sprint will leave them winded, yes, but the mental boost they seem to get from such encounters will carry them many happy miles beyond the last glimpse of the herd.

This time, though, McDougal is not content to simply displace his instincts into a mad rush down the trail. A dozen animals galloping northward are just too enticing for a dozen dogs and we leave the trail in eager pursuit.

Game over: the brake comes on, my full weight upon it as the tongs of it claw the ice. Still we move forward, the dogs leaning and humping into their harnesses, struggling to preserve momentum. At last we stop.

The caribou stop also, a half mile down the bay, in a tight cluster.

"McDougal! Beaver! Gee!" Then, with a threatening growl in my voice, "McDougal! Beaver! Gee, now, gee!"

Beaver, bless his little brain, yanks his recalcitrant partner by the neckline back toward the trail, as if to say, "C'mon boy, give it up. There'll be other days." McDougal shoots me a reproachful glance and yields to Beaver. We regain the trail, I ease up on the brake and we lope ahead, adrenaline still surging through the dogs' blood, not to mention my own and that of 12 caribou.

The surge carries us up the first climb of Pike's Portage. The trail here, in park-like spruce forest, is a deep trough, scooped out and as slick as any bobsled run. Hill after hill rise ahead. I jog behind the sled on the steepest sections, but the load is light and this team is strong.

We reach the first lake, Harry Lake, in just over a half hour. Now the team is winded and the caribou are forgotten. But we have ascended beyond Great Slave and the trail ahead remains smooth and hard. The sky is cloudless and a light northeast breeze has sprung up. The sunlight on snow is blinding when I remove my goggles for a moment to clean them. I wonder how long I could travel today without goggles of some sort as I feel my vest pocket to be sure that my extra pair is still there in its case. Not too long, I don't think, before my retinas would be scorched like a pale tourist on a Florida beach.

A wolf has left his tracks ahead of ours in the snow all the way up from Great Slave and still they lead ahead, a wavering line through the dusting of snow that covers the trail. Evidently they are not as fresh as my eye would like to make them, since the dogs do not constantly sniff them.

Buck is fading. His tugline has gone completely slack and he is occasionally glancing over his shoulder at me, a questioning look in his eyes. He is young, in his first season of running, and one of those dogs for whom the holding of energy in reserve is out of the question. At every morning's start from the yard, he is beside himself. With every opportunity to chase something, be it another dogteam, a snowmobile, or a caribou herd, he is limited only by his own insane desire to pull. I do not try to slow him—neither do I offer him much sympathy when, as now, his muscles scream for a rest, a chance to catch up on oxygen and unload some metabolic wastes.

Age and experience, I figure, will teach him how to pace himself. Meanwhile, so long as he does not actually drag backward on the neckline, I leave him in the team to recover on the run. "Little winded there, eh Buck? Stay with it, chum, you'll come around." Hearing me say his name, he turns to me with a look of pitiable fatigue.

The rest of the dogs are pulling well. Harry Lake's three-mile length falls quickly behind us. We cross a short portage and run down French Lake, about four miles, at the same steady pace. Buck continues to wobble in the traces, but now relief is nearly in sight, for it has been almost two hours since we pulled out of Reliance. According to my habit, on races, training runs, or trips, it is time for the dogs to get a 20-minute break, a snack and a short nap. That should give Buck the recovery time he needs.

At the start of the short trail leading out of French Lake, I gently tell the team, "Whoa now, whoa" and snag a small spruce trunk with the snowhook. The dogs stop with a mild jerk and 12 heads all turn to me at once.

"Take a break, gang," I say, as I open the sled bag and fish out a gunnysack filled with small chunks of frozen beef liver. All eyes upon me, I walk up to the front of the team and toss each dog a snack, working my way back to the sled. Most of them catch the tidbit on the fly and swallow it the instant it enters their mouth.

All the dogs continue to stare at me, studying my every move for the next clue. Sometimes, on a race, a snack does not mean a rest. It's "All right, let's go!" as soon as I get back to the sled. But as they see me sit down on the sled and reach for my own lunch bag and water bottle, they begin shuffling, sniffing, settling down on the snow, licking their paws, urinating and making quick checks to be sure that they haven't somehow missed a piece of the liver somewhere. Within two minutes, 12 dogs are sound asleep on the trail.

Orange juice, still warm from home, dried caribou meat and a square of rich bannock taste good. It feels pleasant to sit down; I am already getting past the tension and uncertainty of the day's beginning. Once the dogs have come 20 miles or so, they are not so much like a team of wild broncos. A rhythm is established. They know that together we are going somewhere and they like that. Today we have made the ritual transition from near-adversaries to traveling partners without any mishaps.

The trees here are all spruce and all small. The start of the tundra is not a distinct line, but a wavering, gradual disappearance of any trees worthy of the name. The trail ahead continues to resemble a highway for us and now, at the height of the day's warmth, it is still pleasantly cold. I am glad that I delayed my departure. Running a team up through here at 50 degrees would have been no fun at all.

It is 3:40 p.m. when I stand and stuff my lunch bag into the sled again. Almost immediately all the dogs are on their feet and Nacho and Troubles have started their impatient high-pitched barking. No lack of enthusiasm here, I think. With a tug on the snowhook and an "All right!" we are off again at a gallop. This time the gallop settles quickly into a more sensible, ground-eating trot.

The trail climbs between French and Acres Lakes, then from Acres to Kipling, Kipling to Burr, Burr to Toura—all named for the paddlers in J. W. Tyrrell's epic

1900 survey east to Hudson Bay. On the portages now the effects of the recent hard blow are obvious—deeply drifted powder obscures the trail in every sheltered spot. Except for a few brief pauses when I walk up to lead McDougal and Beaver to the trail, we move steadily. The wolf tracks are no longer ahead of us. I did not notice where they turned off.

As we cross the windblown snow of Toura Lake, barren hills rise on both sides of us and cairns of stone that mark the summer portage stand in silhouette against the skyline. A raven circles in from the southeast and passes overhead. We are nearly 25 miles from Great Slave Lake now. This bird is the first living creature we have seen in all those miles.

Suddenly, a flock of several dozen rock ptarmigan bursts up from the shore, rousing the dogs into a half-hearted wind sprint. The birds fly swiftly ahead like a storm of huge snowflakes and land on a smooth granite slab to the west. I notice more of them on that warm dark rock, standing there as we pass within 30 yards of them.

Exactly two hours after our last rest stop ended, McDougal and Beaver drop out of sight over a steep hill and are swiftly followed by the rest of the team. I quickly put all my weight on the bar of the brake and get a good grip on the handlebar as the sled pitches forward. A steep short drop, with the brush bow nearly clipping the wheel dogs from behind, and we stop for a rest. We have reached Artillery Lake, a body of water legendary for its role as a passageway to the barrens, the Hanbury-Thelon watershed and—far to the east—Hudson Bay.

The dogs are asleep even more swiftly now than they have been at the first two stops of the day. Still, they have been running as if they could go on forever. It is such a pleasure to travel with them in this way, self-contained and fancy-free, the thoughts of pace and goals and rhythm all pleasant and free from rivalry, competition and strategy.

Yet such thoughts are never completely lost for me when I am with my dogs these days—we are into all of this far too deeply for it to be simply a diversion, an expensive hobby. This trip is a holiday, yes, but it is also a vital renewal of our long-distance training regimen for the experienced dogs and an introduction to it for the young dogs.

We have, regrettably, spent the entire winter training the team for the Canadian Championship Dog Derby, a three-day, 150-mile race that is suited for and dominated by other kinds of dogteams—lean, loping speedsters. All winter, consequently, our runs have been relatively short and the emphasis has constantly been on speed, a loping gait, light loads and fast, hard trails. But our attempt to make Maseratis out of pickup trucks did not succeed. Now, as we hit Artillery and the dogs all curl up for a brief nap, the past winter's efforts are behind us. I am already training the team for next season.

It has been seven years since I first sledded down that hill, two full days out of Reliance, with five dogs scampering to dodge an overloaded toboggan. We were bound then for the Thelon River and on to Baker Lake, or so we thought. The memory of that trip brings a wry smile to me this evening, six hours and nearly 50 miles from home and with 18 miles left for the day. I wonder, as I often have in hindsight, how we ever got as far as we did.

Artillery Lake received its odd name from a captain in the Royal Navy, George Back, who first traveled it while searching for the source of the river that is now named for him. In his brigade of men were four soldiers of the Royal Artillery and he was greatly impressed by their performance on his arduous expedition. This beautiful lake now bears its incongruous name in their honor. Along the lake's 50-mile length, which dramatically straddles the treeline, there are two small cabins still in seasonal use by local trappers. It is for one of these, which belongs to my friends in Reliance, that we are bound this evening.

The sun has now lowered to an oblique angle and as we resume our progress down the length of Artillery, the air suddenly chills me, as if the tundra is pouring out its icy breath in welcome. I have some doubts as to getting all the way to the cabin, since suddenly we have completely lost our packed, defined trail and the dogs are slogging along, weaving among deep drifts topped with a thin breakable crust.

It has never ceased to amaze me what a substantial difference the condition of a trail makes to the dogs and musher of a team. There is no other single factor of the physical environment that has such an effect on a team's progress. It can be −40 degrees or 40 degrees, with a headwind, a tailwind, or absolute calm and if the trail is smooth and hard-packed the dogs will run well—as well as all the other variables allow. But even when everything else about the day and the team's condition is perfect, if the trail is deep, soft, or "punchy"—meaning that the footfalls of the dogs punch through a thin crust into softer snow below—progress slows to a punishing snail's pace.

I have hopes of better conditions just ahead and for once these hopes turn out to be more than just a mental placebo. As we leave the narrow southern fjord and gain the wide expanse of the open lake, the snow conditions quickly improve, firming up to the consistency of a boardwalk. The dogs' pace quickens, the sled begins to clatter and bounce along on the drift tops and my thoughts of getting to the cabin at Rat Lodge are revived.

Rat Lodge is the name given to a pronounced pyramidal point of sand and gravel, like a giant muskrat lodge, visible for miles up and down the lake. It is matched across the lake to the east by an even larger conical island, this one of granite—Beaver Lodge. Years ago a nearby cluster of cabins, a seasonal village of the Chipewyan people, became known as Rat Lodge. Once

I had even seen Rat Lodge pinpointed and labeled on an old and yellowed globe—evidently reflecting someone's desire to put a label on *something* in that wide curve of northern Canada. Now the village is in ruins and the cabin on the point just west of the Rat Lodge has taken up the name.

The sled bangs over the wind-packed snow. The dogs are all pulling strongly, even Buck, but in their gaits now are signs of the weariness that is catching up to them. Some have begun pacing, a lopsided gait in which each pair of legs, the left and the right, move in unison. Some dogs adopt this variation when they get tired in order to utilize a few different muscles. Others, though, are pacers constantly—until *they* tire and break into a trot. The pacing gait is supposedly not as physically efficient as a smooth trot and it is considered to be a negative factor when assessing a dog's athletic potential. Tonight it is mainly Swannie and Buck who have taken it up. They are the youngest dogs in this team and the ones least accustomed to days of loaded sleds, steep climbs and 66-mile itineraries.

The silence, complete all day long, has now become almost eerie. Being back on Artillery Lake, I feel like I have rejoined an old friend, a powerful, mystical friend. The dogs and I are here about as alone as we could ever be. We could travel on this bearing for a full 400 miles, clear to the Arctic Ocean and I would be astounded if we crossed the trail of another person, or came upon a building—even a tent camp—in all those miles. There are no caribou or musk oxen here this evening, no fresh tracks of wolf, wolverine, or fox, no sign of the raven I had seen on Toura Lake.

At 8:05, I give in to the nagging desire to put on some more clothing. The sun has dropped low and is just edging the northwestern horizon. I stop the team, kick in a snowhook and put on a down-filled vest beneath my cotton parka. At last I can take off my dark goggles and this is a welcome change. Everyone in the team gets another small chunk of liver and I take a moment to untwist Fuji's neckline. Although she is now three years old, she has all the mannerisms of a pup and at every pause along the trail she delights in rolling over and over in the snow. By the end of a day's travel her neckline loop and tugline are each so twisted that it is a wonder she can even pull—or breathe, for that matter.

I sit on the sled and sip tea, now lukewarm, from a small thermos bottle. The daylight turns from blinding white to a mellow reddish-gold. Up ahead is the pyramid of Rat Lodge and just to the left of it I can make out a tiny dark square—home for the night.

"Yep," I say aloud, "we're almost there, guys." A dozen pairs of eyes open and regard me sleepily. "O.K., on your feet now, on your feet! Happy dogs! Let's take it on home." My inane cheerleading finds a few takers in the crowd and soon we are underway again, once more leaving our rest spot at an energetic lope.

Now the advantages of running a big team become clear. My friends are forever shaking their heads when they see me depart their cabins with ten or more canine maniacs hitched to the sled. It is crazy then, yes, but not so at the far end of a day like this one, when the synergy of 12 dogs moving together begins to be obvious. The whole is indeed greater than the sum of the parts. Twelve separate dogs each pulling little one-twelfth-scale sleds would be hard-pressed to glide so smoothly across the 60-mile mark of an uphill day. But with 12 dogs working in harmony, the little dark square ahead soon forms itself into a maroon-colored, box-shaped cabin.

"Yip-yip! Let's go home!" I shout in a high-pitched voice that sounds like Mickey Mouse. The trotters shift gears to a slow, tired lope and in a few moments I set two snowhooks side by side in the drift beside the cabin.

As I go about the chores of arrival, the dogs sleep. I find the hidden key, unlock the door, tip a drum of gasoline out of the entrance, chop some ice, start the stove, put the ice on to melt, light the little kerosene heater and secure the picket line with its 12 short chains for the dogs.

Soon the team is tied out, their food is soaking up a few gallons of warm water, the sled is unloaded and I can sit and sip a cool beer that my friends in Reliance had given me. It has been a long day. Setting out so late this morning, I hadn't thought we would get so far, but the dogs have made it look easy. Again my thoughts shift to my last dogteam trip on Artillery and I realize that in the intervening seven years I have learned some things—about dog care mostly and about training and pacing and figuring loads.

I step out to feed the team. A slim crescent moon and a few bright stars join Venus in the evening sky. It is still light enough to do the chores without a headlamp. The team is hungry, understandably so. Their little snacks throughout the day have been burned off quickly—they are morale-boosters more than meals. Now is the time to stoke up their furnaces for the night. A mound of soaked dog food, a healthy piece of lard and a fist-sized chunk of frozen meat go to them all.

They eye my every move even as I put away the sacks of fat and meat, as if *willing* my hand to reach back inside and give them another mouthful. "No such luck, boys," I tell them. "What do you wanna do—eat it all now and then go hungry?" Their looks tell me that this sounds like a perfectly reasonable plan to them.

Smiling, I buckle up the sled bag, take a quick look around at the dimly lit vastness and step into the little cabin. By midnight, my own supper finished, I fall asleep.

Just as I lie down, four or five dogs set up a ferocious barking. Oh hell, I think, somebody's loose. I stumble to the door. Now it is nearly full dark. The team is quiet again. I can see nothing amiss. I go back to bed.

At 4:30 a.m. I roll over in my sleep. Already it is light outside. No, not yet, I think. Then at 6 I figure I may as well get started. Didn't come up here to sleep, I grumble.

Soon some strong coffee is putting the minimum required voltage to my brain, five gallons of warm water flavored with liver and lard are steaming by the cabin door and I am studying the topographic maps of Artillery Lake and Walmsley Lake. I am trying to decide whether to pack up completely and plan to camp elsewhere tonight, or to go out with a light load and return to here.

I am tense again. It is the tension that always comes from heading into new country, especially alone and especially in winter. It is a mood that is careful and demanding. Today it is convincing me to simply head out, explore some new territory and return by the same route to here.

The advantages of doing so are several. First, the dogs, especially the leaders, seem to tire more quickly when they are uncertain of the route, constantly making responses to my shouted commands of gee and haw. If, sometime past mid-day, they are turned homeward on the back trail, they already know what lies in that direction and they run better. Also, the trail home is then a known entity for me; if difficult conditions are encountered they do not come as a bitter surprise in the final hours of the day. I slowly resign myself to the more conservative plan. We will head north ten miles up the lake, cut northwest from there and steer for the south arm of Walmsley Lake. At about 2 p.m., wherever we are, we'll turn back toward Rat Lodge.

It is another clear day. The air is cold but perfectly calm. I cannot believe our good fortune. Neither do I trust it to last very long. After all, the tundra is treeless for some very good reasons, strong winds not least among them. The dogs eagerly lap up their broth and begin working on the corners of their pans in search of congealed lard. I gather up the pans, chop more ice to melt and eat my breakfast.

Just before 9 a.m., eight dogs and I pull away from the cabin, leaving four on the picket line to wonder what in the world is going on. Eight will be plenty of power for a day such as this, I've decided. Twelve dogs with an empty sled and an unfamiliar route would be an invitation to chaos, or even disaster. Four well-rested dogs for tomorrow's run will give us an added boost. I've left the troublemakers behind.

Again today, fresh wolf tracks lead along the route we are taking. So that explains the midnight visitor, I figure. He or she probably joined our trail down the lake somewhere and came past the camp to investigate, as wolves often will. The paw prints are huge, at least half again as big as the ones my biggest dog, Brew, is leaving in the snow beside them.

Again today the light reflected by the snow on lake and tundra is blinding. I wonder how the dogs can avoid snowblindness. I have read accounts of them suffering from it, but never in any veterinary text, only some passing references to it in old memoirs of the North. They do squint and blink in the bright sun, yet it does not seem to bother them to the point of pain or loss of vision.

This country is vast. Landmarks are indistinct, with no clear line of forest to divide the lake from the land. The scale of the map is four miles to the inch. My most frequent navigational errors come from interpretation of this scale. I am forever trying to squeeze the landscape together, to figure we have covered more ground than we actually have, to somehow reduce this bewildering immensity to a size more manageable, more tangible. This morning is no different. No sooner have we climbed away from the lake, the dogs struggling upward over sun-crusted snow and bare patches of rock and lichen, than I realize we have turned west too early. Ahead of us the way is blocked by a grove of substantial spruce, promising deep unpacked snow where the trees have broken the blast of the winds. We cut northeast back to the lake. Someday, maybe, I will grow accustomed to the true dimensions of this land.

Before the day's first rest stop we regain my planned route and once again climb away from Artillery Lake toward the northwest. The land is rolling, interspersed with patches of stunted spruce that grow in every sheltered hollow. The ecologists call this ecosystem by the contradictory name "forest tundra." Ahead are long vistas of white hills, a large lake that bears no name on the map and the serpentine ridge of an esker. As the dogs take a break, I pull out my camera. The counter reads 25, on a roll of 24. So much for photographs.

It has been years, probably, since a dogteam has come this way. Old Louison Drybones was the last of the region's barrenland trappers to depend on dogs. He died three years ago. I try to conjure up an image of him passing this way on an April day. His five dogs would be strung out in a single-file hitch, his toboggan with its canvas cariole snaking along behind, perhaps with him astride the load, a rifle forever slung across his back.

How he would stare at the scene here today! Eight slender dogs arranged in four pairs, a couple of them weighing no more than 45 pounds; the wide sled with its polyethylene bottom, blue nylon cover and varnished laminations of birch, ash and elm. Yet these are only the modern accessories of what has remained essentially unchanged, of what will never change—the relationship of dogteam to musher, the agreement they have struck with one another, the age-old interdependence of human and working animal. Old Louie would not have put it in those words, but I suspect he would have known that despite appearances, nothing has changed here at all.

Time to get back on the move. I put old Louison out of my thoughts for now, glance at my watch and my fancy compass, my precise topographic map and call to my dogs. We move ahead and for the next several hours we pick our way north and west. We jump a single caribou in a rocky draw; the dogs give chase and the tiny bull bounds away over an esker top. I check the map again and again. Finally we climb to the edge of a wide plateau. Here is the divide between the drainage of the Lockhart River, via Artillery Lake and the Hoarfrost

River, via Walmsley. We are 22 miles out from the cabin at Rat Lodge. I lead Beaver and McDougal around in a wide arc. They pick up the trail and quickly leave it again. "No! Gee there, gee! Let's go home!" This last remark seems to surprise them. They look back at me, pick up the pace and head back the way we have come. Walmsley Lake will have to wait for another trip.

Now my tension has eased, but it is still there, a small knot in my gut. It must take years for a person to truly relax in such surroundings as these. Now we are heading back, the sun is high and warm, the route familiar and easy. On Lake 1190 (its elevation marked on the map), we stop and take a long break, nearly two hours. The dogs sprawl on the trail in the warm sunlight. I lie atop the sled and sleep.

When we set off again, Troubles has begun to limp, favoring his right front leg. A short, small dog, he probably post-holed in some deep snow and strained a shoulder muscle. During the rest stop, the injured muscle stiffened. I stop to check him over and as I bend his leg upward, compressing the shoulder, he lets out a sharp, high whine. We move on toward home. I watch him carefully. He continues to keep his tugline tight, a good sign, and adopts an awkward bouncing lope for the remainder of the day.

Toward late afternoon, the cabin is in sight again in the distance. The four dogs there stand against the skyline on the windswept rise. The dogs in the team are tired. They have left some tracks today that no one will ever see. In two months our trail will be gone forever, sublimated out of existence by dry May winds and the endless sun of northern spring.

The clatter of the sled over the rock-hard drifts of the lake has begun to irritate me. I have been banging and bouncing endlessly, it seems. There is a nagging pain in the small of my back, caused in part, I think, by my stubborn insistence on slinging that 30.06 carbine over my shoulder all day yesterday. The rifle now rides on the handlebar of the sled and I try to remember why I brought it. I lower myself to my haunches, to squat awkwardly on the runners, as I have done so many times on stretches of the Iditarod Trail.

I ponder idly over how many miles I have stood on the runners of a dogsled in my life. I lose count somewhere above 13,000 miles. Beaver, one of my main leaders for the last several years, must have traveled 10,000 since I bought him at the age of six. I wonder how far it is around the world at the latitude of 63 degrees north, where we are now. . . .

My back hurts. The sled bounces. "Yip-yip, let's go home!"

We pull up to the cabin; I set the snowhooks and give each dog a friendly pat and a brisk rub. I check all their paws. There will be a need for some booties tomorrow.

I leave the team in harness awhile as I putter around the cabin, melting water, chopping lard and meat. They sleep contentedly. I sit down for a while on the sled, take off my goggles and rub my face with my hands. It has been a good day. The weather has been perfect and there is still no change in sight. The sun has dipped low now and bathes the landscape in alpenglow. The silence is absolute. I put on my goggles again and look carefully up and down the lake. My range of view must be on the order of a hundred square miles. Nothing moves.

I suddenly feel intensely lucky to be here, to know such silence, such space and freedom. Good dogs, warm pure sunlight, clean air, white snow. I think, as I often do, of the words of the Danish-Inuit explorer Knud Rasmussen: "Give me winter, give me dogs and you can have the rest."

I take the team from harness, give Troubles a little aspirin and a rubdown, feed the dogs, chop ice, eat supper. At dusk I take a short walk up the sandy peninsula toward the north. The air is cooling rapidly. I stand still for a moment, waiting . . . then I turn and go back indoors.

By the hissing light of the gas lamp I sit up late reading a book I have found on the shelf, the story of the attempted assassination of the Pope.

Another day begins clear, calm and cold. By 9 a.m. the cabin is locked, the sled is loaded and the dogs that need them are wearing their booties. I gingerly begin harnessing the team.

If I am to lose them on this journey, now would be the likely time. They are eager, fresh and pointed toward home. Down the lake lie 18 miles of free, fast running. The only thing I can tie the sled to is a flimsy spruce pole meant to serve only as an antenna mast. With nine of the dogs in harness and three more to add, they begin to bark and whine and paw the snow. I double-check all the anchors, two snowhooks and a snubline tied off to the pole, talk to them in firm, calm tones and wind up the picket cable from its far end toward the sled. When I come to the last three dogs, still hooked to the cable, I breathe easier.

Now the danger is nearly past. I can finish everything within reach of a desperate lunge toward the sled. Grayling, Buck and Nacho all go into their places in the team, the picket line is stowed and we are away. I breathe a huge sigh of relief as Rat Lodge dwindles to a tiny speck behind the careening sled and galloping dogs.

Steadily we retrace our trail of two days before. On the portage out of Toura Lake, we cross the fresh trail of a wolverine shuffling and circling among the rocks of a steep hillside. Then we jump a group of 40 or more ptarmigan, who sit clucking and cooing to us from ten feet away. With them just past, the team suddenly catches a fresh whiff of something unseen and leaves the trail in a frenzy. We run in wide circles for what seems like 20 minutes as I argue stubbornly with my equally stubborn lead dogs. Finally, my voice gruff and threatening, Beaver and McDougal acquiesce and we continue down the trail.

Soon the tracks of a couple dozen caribou appear—they had been up another arm of the lake, evidently moving north and east, but had been using our trail for seven or eight miles. It is as if all the creatures of the tundra are waiting here at treeline—waiting for this last lone human and his dogs to get clear of their country. Well, I think, it's all yours now till summer time.

We cross French and Harry Lakes and make the swift descent to Great Slave. I revel in the exhilaration of that run, with its curving downhills and a solid, icy trail, the vistas of Charlton and McLeod Bays spread out below. I look up as we come close to Glacier Creek and see a bald eagle swinging in lazy circles high overhead— a sure sign of spring.

The dogs know they are bound for home. I stop briefly in Reliance to visit with Roger and Theresa and set off across McLeod Bay for the Hoarfrost.

I sing to the dogs in a horrible nasal imitation of Willie Nelson. They run faster, in a desperate effort to escape. We pull into the yard amidst a cacaphony of greeting from the dogs who have been left behind and a cheerful wave from Bruce, who has been looking after the homestead.

We have come 180 miles in the three days since we pulled out of here. There will be many more days of dog driving this season, even into June on the candled ice of Great Slave, but the trips from now on will be short and the teams small.

The dogs roll and tussle with each other in their yard, glad to be home.

The roar of the falls at the mouth of the river is clear and strong in the stillness, much louder than it has been through the long winter.

GLOSSARY—SOME DOG MUSHING TERMS

ALASKAN HUSKY—any sled dog with a genetic background traced to Alaskan dogs. Not a "pure" breed.

ATTITUDE—the desire and drive to run and pull, vital in sled dogs.

BARRENS, BARRENLANDS—terms common in northern Canada describing treeless country or tundra.

BASKET—the load-carrying portion of a dogsled.

BASKET SLED—a type of dogsled wherein the load rests on a raised platform of wooden slats supported by stanchions.

BEARGREASE—the John Beargrease Sled Dog Marathon, a 480-mile race held each year in January along the north shore of Lake Superior.

BEAVER MEAT—meat trimmed from the carcasses of beavers that have been trapped for their pelts; an excellent food for racing dogs since it is very rich and palatable.

BOOTIES—cloth or leather stockings about 3½ inches tall that protect the dogs' feet from abrasive snow, ice or gravel. Required equipment on all long-distance races and frequently used in training.

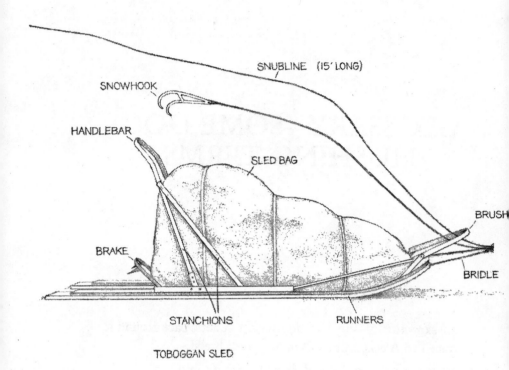

SNUBLINE (15′ LONG)

SNOWHOOK

HANDLEBAR

SLED BAG

BRUSH

BRAKE

BRIDLE

STANCHIONS

RUNNERS

TOBOGGAN SLED

BRAKE—any device, usually with a metal tooth or claw, that attaches to the rear of a dogsled and that slows the sled when the musher steps on it.

BRIDLE—the loop of heavy rope or cable by which the gangline and pulling force of the dogs are joined to the front of a dogsled.

BROKEN, UNBROKEN TRAIL—"breaking" a trail usually connotes making the first passage along a route through deep, fresh snow. The same trail is often "broken" many times each winter (once after each storm).

BRUSH BOW—a stout curved piece of wood, metal or plastic that extends forward from the front edge of a dogsled and acts as a fender.

CARIOLE—the canvas covering that supports and covers the load on a traditional wooden toboggan sled.

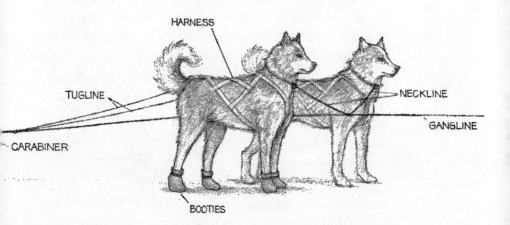

HARNESS

TUGLINE

NECKLINE

GANGLINE

CARABINER

BOOTIES

CHECKER—the race official responsible for overseeing the arrival and departure of teams from a checkpoint.

CHECKPOINT—a designated site along a race trail where teams must sign in and out on a roster sheet. Often a place for resting, dog care, veterinary checks, and re-supply.

CHEECHAKO—the term used in the Yukon-Alaska gold rush for newcomers and inexperienced northern travelers.

COMMAND LEADER—a lead dog capable of following precisely the voice commands of a musher to steer a team along a specific route or heading.

DOG BOX—the compartment for one or two dogs built onto the back of a dog truck.

DOG TRUCK—any truck or van modified to provide carrying places for a dogteam and its gear.

DOG YARD, LOT—the home kennel where sled dogs are tethered or fenced.

DROPPED DOG, DOG DROP—these refer to the option of leaving dogs off from a racing team at designated points, usually because they have become tired or have been slightly injured. They are cared for by race personnel and are returned to the musher after the race.

FOOD DROP—the official resupply of provisions and gear for all dogs and mushers, arranged prior to major wilderness races such as the Iditarod and Yukon Quest.

GALLOP—a high-speed gait in which a dog's feet strike the ground or snow with a rapid, four-beat rhythm, as contrasted to the slower, three-beat "lope."

GANGLINE—the main line that transfers the power of the team from the tuglines back to the sled (see illustration page 235).

GEE—the most common command directing a lead dog to turn to the right.

GET UP!—a common command to a dog or an entire team, encouraging them to pick up speed or pull harder.

GREENHORN—a beginner or novice musher.

HANDLEBAR—the horizontal rail at the back of a dogsled, which the musher grasps while riding or pedaling.

HANDLER—a person who assists a racing musher in all aspects of preparation and performance during a race; i.e., the "pit crew."

HARNESS—any style of device, usually made of padded nylon webbing, that a sled dog wears and through which its pulling power is transferred to the lines leading back to the sled.

HAW—the most common command directing a lead dog to turn to the left.

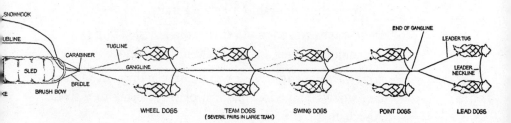

HEADLAMP—the electric light worn strapped to the forehead of a musher to illuminate the dogs and trail ahead at night; usually powered by a battery pack on the belt or on the strap of the headlamp itself.

HEAT—a slang term for estrus, the fertile reproductive season of female dogs.

HIKE!—a common start-up command for a dogteam. Mush! is rarely used.

HOUND—a generic term for breeds of dogs not commonly thought of as sled dogs, but commonly bred into racing huskies: greyhound, saluki, coon hound, etc.

IDITAROD—the Iditarod Trail Sled Dog Race, a 1,200-mile race run each year between Anchorage and Nome, Alaska. The name originates from a native word meaning "distant place." This in turn became the name of a gold-mining town and the trail leading to it.

INTERIOR—the central portion of the state of Alaska, away from the coasts.

JINGLER—a noisemaker used by mushers to encourage dogs to run faster.

LEADER, LEAD DOG(s)—the dog(s) running at the front of the team, farthest from the sled, and thus determining the team's pace and direction of travel. See **COMMAND LEADER**.

LINE-BREEDING, IN-BREEDING—terms used to describe matings of dogs already closely related, e.g., parents to offspring, cousins to each other, etc. Often arranged in order to strengthen desirable inherited traits.

LONG-DISTANCE RACE—in this book, any sled dog race run continuously over a course 400 miles or more in length.

LOPE—a gait, slightly slower than a gallop, in which a dog's paws move in a pattern of three beats to a stride. Also called a canter.

MALAMUTE—a pure breed of husky known for large size, thick fur and a stocky, wolfish appearance. Uncommon in racing dogteams.

MANDATORY GEAR—the items a team is required to carry in the sled on a long-distance race, such as a sleeping bag, snowshoes, axe, dog booties, headlamp, etc.

MANDATORY LAYOVER—a required rest stop that each team must make during a race, for a designated number of hours and sometimes at a designated checkpoint.

MIDDLE-DISTANCE RACE—in this book, any sled dog race run continuously over a course 100 to 400 miles in length.

MOUSE BOOTS, OR MICKEY MOUSE BOOTS—rubber, heavily insulated boots, usually white, worn by many mushers.

MUKLUKS—native-style winter footgear, often with a moosehide or sealskin foot and a tall canvas upper, thickly insulated with wool liners.

MUSHER—the person driving a team of sled dogs; also "driver."

NECKLINE—the short line that joins a dog's collar to the gangline; under tension only if the dog is pulling far off to one side.

OVERFLOW—saturated snow or slush caused by lake or river water rising up and flooding existing ice.

PACE—a two-beat gait in which the dog's paws and legs on each side move as a pair; not a desirable gait for racing dogs.

PADS—the five bottom surfaces on a dog's paw, free of hair and covered by tough skin (four "toe-pads" and a center "foot-pad").

PEDALING—the one-legged pushing gait used by mushers to help move the sled along.

PICKET LINE—a long chain or cable to which dogs are tethered by short lengths of chain or cable when camped or resting.

POINT DOG(s)—the dog(s) running next in the team behind the leader(s). In Alaska these are sometimes called the SWING DOGS.

PORTAGE—any trail used in summer or winter to connect two bodies of water.

PRESSURE RIDGE—a wall of ice, sometimes over 10 feet tall, caused by the expansion or movement of lake, river or sea ice.

PROMOTIONAL MATERIAL—a small packet of letters or mementoes that teams carry on long races; these items are then sold as souvenirs by the race organization.

PURSE—the total prize money to be awarded in a given race.

RACE MARSHALL, CHIEF JUDGE—the final authority on rules and decisions at a sled dog race.

RACING SLED—any light, fast sled designed for speed rather than load-carrying.

RUFF—the fur trimming around the edge of a parka hood.

RUNNERS—the two long up-curved surfaces on which a basket sled or a modern toboggan sled runs. Also refers to the covering strips of plastic or steel that actually touch the snow or ice surface.

SAMOYED—a pure breed of white husky named for a tribe of native people in Siberia; very uncommon in modern dogteams.

SIBERIAN—the pure breed of Siberian husky, which commonly forms a *part* of the background of modern sled dogs.

SKIDOO, SNOW MACHINE—common slang terms for a snowmobile.

SKIJORING—from the Scandinavian word describing a skier being pulled directly by one or more harnessed dogs with no sled.

SLED BAG—the cloth covering that attaches within the basket of a dogsled to contain and cover the load. Usually closed on top by buckles or a zipper.

SNACK—a brief stop along the trail at which the dogs are given a small bit of meat or fish.

SNOWHOOK, HOOK—a heavy metal anchor with two curved prongs attached to the dogteam via the front of the bridle. Used to anchor and restrain the team at virtually every stop along the trail. Can be hooked around a tree trunk, kicked into packed snow, or pounded into glare ice.

SNUBLINE—a length of stout rope that, like the snowhook, connects directly to the dogteam via the bridle. Used to anchor the team to posts or trees, especially when starting out on a run.

SPONSOR—an individual, firm or institution providing material and/or financial support to a racing team, an expedition, or an event.

SPRINT RACE, SPRINT DOG, SPRINT MUSHER—in this book, a sled dog race is called a "sprint" if it involves distances under 100 miles and repeated daily runs over the same trail.

STANCHION—an upright supporting member in the frame of a dogsled.

SWING DOG(s)—the dog(s) running behind the point dog(s). The terms "swing" and "point" are used differently by various mushers.

TIE-OUT—a cable, like a picket line, used to tether dogs at campsites and rest stops.

TOBOGGAN SLED—a dogsled with a wide flat bottom of wood or plastic, used often for freighting, racing, and traveling in deep snow.

TOGGLE—a short length of carved wood that slips through a loop in the tugline and is attached to the dog's harness. Brass snaps can also be used to make this connection.

TRAINING CART—any sort of wheeled vehicle used as a substitute for a dogsled on roads, lanes, or trails.

TROT—the prevalent gait of long-distance sled dogs. A smooth, fluid movement with diagonally opposite legs and paws moving in unison; i.e., front left with rear right, front right with rear left.

TUGLINE, OR TUG—the 36" to 56" length of rope that joins a dog's harness to the gangline. Tension on the tugline indicates how hard a dog is pulling.

VET—a veterinarian.

WHOA—the most common command used to slow and stop a dogteam.

WHEEL DOG(s)—the dog(s) closest to the sled at the rear of the team.

WHITEFISH—a common fish of northern lakes and rivers that is excellent food for racing and working sled dogs.

YEARLING—a dog approximately 10 to 23 months old.

YUKON QUEST, QUEST—an annual long-distance race run between Fairbanks, Alaska, and Whitehorse, Yukon, via Dawson City. About 1,000 miles in length, with a limit of 12 dogs per team.

YUKON STOVE—any type of small, square portable woodstove used to heat temporary camps or cabins.

COLOPHON

Designed by Moonlit Ink, Madison, WI
Illustrations and maps by Luann Roberts, Madison, WI
Type set in Bembo by Impressions Inc., Madison, WI
Printed and bound by The Banta Co., Menasha, WI
Published by NorthWord Press Inc., Minocqua, WI

FORT RAE

NORTH ARM

GREAT SLA

FORT

FORT PROVIDENCE

HAY RIVER

ENTERPRISE

STEEN RIVER

SCALE

0   50   100 MILES